Libertarian Education

by Bill Anderson

MY LIBERTARIAN EDUCATION

Copyright Bill Anderson, 2024

All rights reserved. Except for brief passages quoted in newspaper, magazine, radio, television or online reviews, no portion of this book may be reproduced, distributed, or transmitted in any form by any means, electronic or mechanical, including photocopying, recording, or information storage or retrieval system, without the prior written permission of the author.

ISBN 979-8-218-46726-5

Manufactured in the United States of America
First printing July 2024

This is for Candace, an exemplary voluntaryist.

Contents

Preface	i
Arcadia	1
Arcadia II	6
During the War	11
Grief	16
Wasn't That a Time?	20
Mentors	32
Mentors II	37
Business	48
Business II	57
Why I am Not a Social Democrat	63
Education	70
John Kimball	75
Those Social Issues	81
Confronting the State	87
Confronting the State II	96
Saving the Books	102
"What Did You Do During the Coup, Daddy?"	110
Narratives	115
Appendix	118

Preface

This is a political memoir. While it doesn't rise to the level of such classics of the genre as those by Henry Adams, Lincoln Steffens, Albert Jay Nock, Whittaker Chambers and Malcolm X, it may be of interest to readers curious about its time and to taxonomists of ideologies.

The education is "libertarian" in two senses: it was acquired almost entirely outside classrooms, and a deep appreciation of liberty was its result.

*

Some names were changed in chapters 4, 5, and 15.

*

Candace, Buzz Anderson, Doug Kaplan, Rahn Garcia, and Steven Woodside read all or parts of the manuscript in various stages of completion. I thank them for their valuable suggestions and for encouraging me and sometimes worrying about me.

My editor, Rob Bignell, helped me to embrace the comma and pointed out the places where I would lose readers.

Arcadia

Riding down country roads in the open air in the back of my father's flatbed Ford, I could name the families who owned the orchards and fields we passed – Caceba's prunes, Taminelli's peaches, Kowiki's strawberries, Mabie's tomatoes, Frost's prunes, French's pears, Gonzales's tomatoes, Tomamatsu's cherries, and our prunes and walnuts. The Kowiki's strawberry stand, a whitewashed shack with a big red strawberry painted on the side, must have been successful, because they bought a slice of my father's orchard and built a full produce market. We could walk to it, just as we could walk through our orchard in the other direction to buy eggs from the Owens family, who kept chickens.

The Central Valleys of the San Joaquin and the Sacramento may have contained large agribusinesses and gigantic water projects, but our Santa Clara Valley, one of the many small valleys tucked into the coastal mountains of California, was the home of the smallholder—the yeoman farmer, though we didn't use these English terms. We called our farms "ranches," a holdover from Spanish days.

Here, immigrants and their descendants from every European nation from Armenia to Ireland, worked together, were friends, married one other. One hundred years earlier, the Native Americans had been treated abominably, even murderously. And for a century after the Gold Rush Asians had sometimes suffered from legal disabilities and worse. But by the 1950s, the Valley looked like a successful melting pot. There was no black/white issue simply because there were so few Blacks in rural California. Blacks were so rare that seeing a black person was something a child might remark on at the end of the day, though all summer long we listened to the radio rooting for Willie Mays.

People were not far removed from the immigrant generation. At least one of my ancestors had been a farm laborer in California. Two of my Swedish ancestors had been domestic servants in San Jose. When we saw the struggles of new arrivals from Oklahoma or Mexico or elsewhere we often saw our own family's past, and we wished them well. A major determinant of economic success was simply how long your family had been in this wonderful place.

Not everyone owned a farm, of course, but the presence of so many small farmers gave society an egalitarian cast. Farmers and their families worked alongside the seasonal hired help, performing the same tasks. You could not tell at a glance who owned the land. There was no marked out elite; any boundary one could use to define it was too permeable. There was no economic underclass, by which I mean a critical mass of dysfunctional families. There was no despised group.

Of course, there sometimes was conflict, but social conflict usually occurs as part of the aftermath of politicians starting wars or bankers starting depressions, not from the viciousness of the people.

Each summer from 1962 through 1969 we (I, my brother, a cousin or two and sometimes a friend) picked prunes for the three weeks or so until school started. We didn't have a mechanical shaker. Someone went ahead of us with a pole that had a hook on the end of it. Each limb was grasped with the hook, and you gave it a shake to bring down fruit. It was an art. Too weak a shake and not enough fruit would come down. Too vigorous a shake, and green fruit would come down. The green fruit was supposed to be left on the tree to ripen before the next picking of the orchard a few days later. The fruit was called the "French Prune." No one ever called them "plums;" that name was reserved for the Santa Rosas and Satsumas that were grown elsewhere. We went on our hands and knees to gather the prunes and put them into buckets. The buckets were then dumped into wooden boxes, the boxes were lifted by hand onto the flatbed (which gave my father powerful arms) and driven to the dehydrator to be dried into dried prunes. The dehydrator was owned by the Sunsweet Growers Cooperative. When I was younger my father and his cousin had had their own dehydrator.

I was glad we had an orchard rather than strawberries or tomatoes. Picking those meant being in the hot sun. In the orchard we were in shade much of the time. A couple of rows away there would be a Mexican family picking with us. My father did not hire individuals for the harvest; he would hire an extended family, and they would decide who showed up. Often there were children the same age as us, 9 to 18, picking alongside their siblings and cousins. My father didn't "boss" them. The pickers were paid by the box, rather than by the hour. It was up to the family to decide what to expect from each member. My father just counted the filled boxes, made sure they didn't contain green fruit, and loaded them onto the truck, sometimes with our help. Every now and then one of the Mexicans would pick 40 boxes of fruit in a day, and we would be in awe of that achievement. One year a neighbor lady born in Portugal picked with us, practicing her English along with working. A generation earlier many of the pickers would have been refugees from the Dust Bowl. A generation before that some of the pickers would have been from Japan. Most social mobility happens from one generation to the next. Many a teenager who picked prunes went on to achieve success.

My mother's family lived in San Jose in an Italian neighborhood. Most of her neighbors spoke Italian at home, and many of them worked in the canneries canning peaches and pears. My mother's Irish American father worked in the canneries too, printing can labels during the good times and shoveling peach pits when the Great Depression and too much alcohol took their toll.

*

In 1969 we harvested our last crop. We had no regrets about this. Farming is hard work. We had moved on. Most of the farmers in North America who left the land were not dispossessed. They left the land because farmers became so productive that fewer of them were needed. Since 1962, we had also been in the motel business in Capitola. Our land went for housing as Silicon Valley was built out.

Every now and then I hear someone say that, since the Santa Clara Valley was good farm land, it should have remained farmland forever. I've tried to counter with arguments about the price system and the theory of comparative advantage, etc., but with little success. I would point out that sometimes the most productive course overall is to plant your crop in the second-best field, but people don't want to hear this. It involves sums, and people want poetry.

Wendell Berry, the novelist, poet, and farmer from Kentucky, even wrote a poem entitled "Santa Clara Valley" in which he decried the transition of the Santa Clara Valley into industry and housing. In this poem the evil "stranger with money" assaults the "remembered homestead, orchard and pasture." But the people who came to the valley simply wanted to realize their dreams and aspirations for a better life, as did the farmers who sold to them. A few of the farmers even used the money they received to develop larger farms in the next valley.

Nonfarmers may derive pleasure from seeing their farmer

neighbors tied to a particular piece of land, imagining us to be enjoying some kind of mystic union with it. But it is not a particular plot of land that we love the most. It is our liberty to do what we will with what is ours that we cherish.

Arcadia II

When I walked into Maverick's liquor store in Capitola, he wasn't at the front counter. I could see him way in the back eating his lunch and reading the paper. Maverick seemed ancient to me, as I was seven or eight, while he was probably in his sixties with a ruddy complexion and gray hair coming out from under his beret. He walked to the front slowly, like he had arthritis or a hangover, and when he got to the counter, I laid out my penny to buy one piece of penny candy. The next time I did this, a couple of days later, he glowered at me and said, "Don't disturb me if you're only going to spend one cent!" So, I took my patronage to Heskett's variety store around the corner. There was always a clerk on duty at Heskett's counter, and they had a better selection of penny candy anyway. For one cent I could buy a piece of faux candied watermelon or a wax cylinder about the size of a pencil, from which you bit off the end to drink the swallow of Kool-Aid inside.

This first participation in commerce taught me that the customer determines what is produced, that sellers care about their costs, and that competition gives you more and better choices. Later, as penny candy disappeared, I learned about inflation.

Capitola is a small beach town nestled in a cove on Monterey Bay. The businesses by the beach along the Esplanade have always been geared to tourists. When I was young there was a merry-go-round whose proprietor would give my little sister free rides, probably to help drum up business. You could rent a beach umbrella and buy a snow cone or cotton candy at one of the hamburger places. A lot of space was devoted to games like pinball or pokerino or skee-ball. Skee-ball is like bowling, except a ramp carries your ball up to where it becomes airborne and then falls into a bucket worth a certain number of points. After each game you get tickets based on your point total. These could be redeemed at the gift case. I'm sure that if you had a lot of points you could get some cheap dishes or a mug, but my brother and I always spent our tickets immediately on candy cigarettes or Chinese handcuffs. Today the businesses on the Esplanade are all restaurants and bars. Skee-ball no longer pays the rent.

Up until 1967, you could stand on the street one block back from the beach and think you were in a small town in the San Joaquin Valley. There was a drug store, a hardware store, two grocery stores, a used clothing store run by the Episcopal church, a barber shop, and a few restaurants. Each business was small. There were no chain stores. In each you could see the owner at work. Mr. Robinson would be mixing his drugs at his drug store. In Nussbaum's market, Bernice Nussbaum would work the single cash register while her husband Alger worked the meat counter. The Jacobs family, husband, wife and daughter, ran their movie theater, which looked like it was an old converted Quonset hut. For 25 cents, a kid could see a double feature, a cartoon and a newsreel. You could stay in your seat and see the main feature twice if you wanted to.

The owner was the cook at each restaurant. Babe Yablanovich would be standing over the fryer at his place, The Bandstand. His French fries were local favorites. (His secret: they were fried in lamb lard he got from his Slavonian friends in Watsonville.) We would see Thelma Juhl cooking in the kitchen at Mac's Patio (Mac, deceased, had been her first husband) as her new husband, Ole, a rotund and genial Dane with a thick accent, came out to greet us and show us a table. "You know, Frank," Ole would say to my father, "a Swede is a Dane without a brain!" and smile broadly at his own joke. I remember Mr. Benias behind the counter of his restaurant with his apron on regretfully telling us,

"The day I left Greece to come to America, my father took me aside and said, 'Son, there's something I want you never to forget.' But for the life of me, I can't remember what it was he said."

Mrs. Lino had a horseshoe-shaped counter along with a few tables at her small restaurant, but there would be a line of people outside waiting for her no-nonsense food like pork chops and a slice of homemade pie. Mrs. Lino had only one waitress, Pearl, who was rather outspoken. In 1930s and 1940s, movies there would sometimes be a waitress like Pearl in the cast – someone totally devoid of servility who gave it back double if she got any guff. I suppose this character would be written into the script to reassure the audience that the average American could never become an obedient Nazi or Communist. I thought of Pearl a few years ago when my wife and I stayed at a five-star hotel (we got in on a group rate.) After a couple days, the obsequiousness of the staff began to grate on me. If fate suddenly made me an English Lord with servants, I'd run screaming from the manor in a week looking for a café with a waitress like Pearl.

*

I am always interested in books about anarchism, so a few years ago when I saw James C. Scott's book *Two Cheers for Anarchism* among the stacks of college-assigned books at the Literary Guillotine bookstore, I picked it up and leafed through it. Hitting immediately on a passage that displayed cringeworthy ignorance of free markets, I set it aside and sighed, "Just another academic social scientist who needs to learn the ABCs of economics and traditional liberalism. No wonder a U.C. Santa

Cruz prof assigned him."

A couple of months later, I picked up another copy of the book and looked at it more closely. There is great stuff in it on resistance to war, and he draws profound lessons from ordinary things like crosswalks and playgrounds. But I was completely sold on the book when I dipped into the chapter entitled: "Two Cheers for the Petty Bourgeoisie." What follows this scrap of Marxist jargon is a sixteen-page love letter to small business.

Scott checks off the benefits small businesses provide to the surrounding neighborhood: small businesses are alert to what the customer wants and eager to provide good service; they develop a convivial personal relationship with many of the locals; and they are "eyes and ears" on the street, scanning for crime and disorder. But it is the yearning many people feel for the freedom that comes with self-employment that Scott focuses on. Certainly the self-employed are constrained by the wants of their customers, but they avoid overt, minute-by-minute supervision by bosses with rule books. We all yearn for some freedom in the use of our time, some scope for decision making, and membership in a human-scale voluntary community. In our popular culture you can see this yearning in Hallmark Channel movies, where the heroine, in the process of finding Mr. Right, often decides she wants to live in a small town and own a small business.

*

Some years ago, I found this passage in a book review article in the Wall Street Journal (Alas, I didn't write down the name of the author.):

"Running a good shop is a service to one's community, of much greater value, in my view, than the work of two hundred social workers, five hundred psychotherapists, and a thousand second-rate poets – and more honorable than the efforts of the vast majority of the members of Congress."

*

Red was a customer who came into our Auto Parts store regularly to get parts for his truck or equipment. He and his son had a farm where they grew flowers. Red was in his seventies. He wore a white cowboy hat and had the weathered face and sinewy arms of someone used to manual labor.

Red was on Medicare, but he hadn't signed up for Social Security. When a clerk questioned him about this, he explained, "I don't believe in goddamn Social Security." I sometimes think of Red as the Last True American.

One Sunday morning at 10 AM, when we opened, Red came in to our parts store and seated himself on a stool at the end of the parts counter. He chatted with me and our two salespeople when business was slow. He chatted with customers who came in, some of whom he knew. On weekends we would sometimes have a small TV on a shelf tuned in to a game, and Red watched that for a while. He stayed on his stool for five hours until we closed at 3PM. Red's wife had recently died, and he could hardly bear to be home alone with memories of her, so he spent the day with us.

During the War

World War II ended in our kitchen in 1962. Up until that time, we saved our bacon grease in a tin can above the stove. The fat and gristle of leftover roast beef would be fed into a heavy meatgrinder we pulled out of the cupboard to make hash. Spam was sometimes the meat on the menu. Or thin slices of very salty dried beef that came from a jar would be creamed and served on toast, called a "shingle" (as in, "something on a shingle.") We were told to eat our Brussels sprouts because "English children had lived on them during the war." This changed when we moved from the farm to Capitola and started to live "high on the hog," as my father would say.

The past fades slowly. In 1960, the silverware in our school cafeteria was presumably "war surplus;" it had "U.S.N." stamped on the handles. Military-style crew cuts held up in front with a gob of Butch Hair Wax lingered into the 1950s, finally replaced by hair parted on the side. I remember when my mother started parting my hair. Each morning in the kitchen before I went out the door she carefully combed a straight line between the northbound and southbound strands. I suppose I part my hair on the left because she was right-handed.

My father once told me that he felt he could talk to me as if I remembered the 1940s. I don't, of course, but listening to my parents, my aunts and uncles and their friends and my school teachers and watching movies and reading books and listening to music and reading popular magazines from 1941 as part of a college assignment, I absorbed the war as surely as Americans born in 1872 absorbed the Civil War as part of their world.

Three of my uncles were in it. My Uncle Carl, who had studied electronics, was a radar repairman in the Solomon Islands. My Uncle Woody, whose father had been a telephone man, was put in a front-line job in the Signal Corps. My Uncle Bob, who worked for Kraft Foods, served in the Quartermaster Corps and landed in France around D-Day plus ten. They were all fortunate to have had something that helped keep them out of the infantry. But only a few could be so fortunate. There weren't enough young men whose job skills involved killing to fill all the combat assignments.

One of my grade school teachers spoke of the war as if it were the great adventure of his life. Apparently, he got to see the South Pacific in assignments of relative safety. Everyone's war was different. The father-in-law of my wife's cousin was in the Polish Cavalry in 1939. He spent half the war as a guest of Stalin and half the war as a guest of Hitler. On the other hand, one friend of our family did his entire service at the Presidio in San Francisco.

My Uncle Woody was unlucky enough to land on Omaha Beach on June 7, 1944. Two of his buddies were killed that day. He didn't talk about the war much. Unlike the veterans you see on TV who go back to the places where they fought, he never wanted to see Europe again. My Uncle Bob was captain of an all-colored unit. The army was segregated then, and Blacks were in noncombat units with white officers. (Congress didn't want Blacks coming home after the war with medals or rank.) He got along well with his men. They were probably relieved the first time they heard his California accent; he had no experience of segregation. Some of his men kept in touch with him and visited him after the war. Each unit of the Quartermaster Corps took its turn collecting dead bodies. My uncle thought this was on par with combat as a traumatic experience. When the war ended, men who had been in combat were sent home first. The

Quartermaster Corps stayed on for the occupation of Germany and to help feed people, so it was a while before he came home, and he had the chance to see some of the devastation caused by bombing.

*

"So, what did your father do during the war?" I've taken to telling people that he learned to speak Spanish. The "Okies" had gone into the military or the defense industries, and the Japanese were in internment camps, so Mexican braceros were brought into the United States to work on the farms, and my father was given an agricultural exemption to work with them. He was a farmer. He had no brothers to work the farm, and my grandfather had been confined to a wheelchair for years. Even so, one member of the draft board voted against my father's exemption (Sell the farm and go fight!)

My father joked about his experience with the draft board. (" They took one look at me and said, 'Who sent you here? The enemy?") But I wonder, did anyone express resentment at my father's good fortune? Did he feel self-conscious going into town young, healthy, and in civilian clothes? Mexican nationals (the Zoot Suiters, for example) were sometimes targeted by envious Americans who had been drafted. What about him? All he ever said was that he and everyone worked hard during the war. He took a second job as a courier for a photo company. When the Tomamatsus, who lived across the lane, were sent to an internment camp, he farmed their land too, per an agreement they made with my grandfather – a fair rental agreement that didn't take advantage and that returned the farm to them in good condition after the war. Mr. Tomamatsu always respected my grandfather for that, and the respect was mutual, sometimes expressed in the Japanese manner with mutual bowing. My mother's impression of the Japanese internment was that no one in California thought that the Japanese Americans they knew were disloyal, but few were willing to question anything the government called a "war measure."

Reminders of the war would crop up unexpectedly. There was a man in Capitola who walked the Esplanade talking into an imagined radio about enemy positions. The surfers left him alone. I saw another man react in sudden terror to a baked potato placed in his hand. His face contorted in fear, he shouted "It's a grenade!" The people around him swiftly reassured him that it was only a potato. These men were "nervous from the service," which sounds rather jolly compared with "Post Traumatic Stress Disorder." One of my business school professors, a German, began his lecture one day by telling us about being in an air raid shelter in Dresden when the city was fire bombed. I imagine it was on the thirtieth anniversary. "Even the SS man," he told us, "was on his knees praying."

Questions about the morality of the war tend to focus on the atomic bombing of Hiroshima and Nagasaki. Some claim that these acts were justified because they "saved American lives." Well, if "saving American lives" was our war-aim in the Pacific, we should have negotiated a peace the day after Pearl Harbor, as Congresswoman Jeannette Rankin wanted to do. Absent the war, we would have escaped its legacies: the military industrial complex, the C.I.A., high tax rates and income tax withholding, the world on the fiat dollar standard, and the empire of bases. And there would have been no U.S. wars in Korea or Vietnam, unless we could have arranged for Kim Il Sung or Ho Chi Minh to bomb Pearl Harbor.

*

We had no relatives killed in the war, or close friends either, as far as I know. In this we were lucky. Once my mother and I leafed through her high school yearbook and she pointed out the picture of one young man after another saying "He was killed in the war...he was killed in the war..." There were a lot of them, but she pointed them out without comment or emotion. The war was not questioned. I did not question the political decisions that led to it until I discovered some of the writings of the historical revisionists when I was 23 or 24 and became interested in America First. I once asked my father if he could sing "I Didn't Raise My Boy to Be a Soldier." He tried hard to remember the lyrics and the melody, but couldn't, and his voice soon trailed off to nothing. The effect was less subversive than my aunt sharing a naughty lyric from "Roll Me Over."

Theirs was a stoic generation. They knew that someone else always had it worse. My parents never complained about the war years, except once when my father said, "Sometimes the only alcohol we could get was Mexican beer."

One day in the 1970s, my father discovered a jar of Postum in the supermarket and bought it. Postum is a kind of ersatz coffee made of toasted grain and molasses. He brewed us each a cup and I tried it. "We used to drink this during the war," he said. It wasn't too bad, but he never bought it again. Kraft Foods stopped making it in 2007.

Grief

Mr. Morrison was voting for Lyndon Johnson. The election was our seventh-grade teacher's favorite topic that autumn of 1964. He even made it a writing assignment. Most of the students were for Johnson or didn't care, but Debbie Schable and I mounted a doughty defense of Barry Goldwater. I'm sure we got the worst of the arguments. The only materials we had were a couple of leaflets and, after all, we were just kids, and Mr. Morrison was a grown up.

There was one thing Morrison said that I distinctly remember because he said it in a quiet and earnest voice: "I was too young to be in World War II, but I was old enough to know many families that had young men serving. I remember their fear. I remember their grief. I don't want to see that again, and that's why I'm voting for Lyndon Johnson."

*

Soldiers in Vietnam didn't just write letters home. You could also send your family a tape recording. I remember when Bill Mabie and his wife came to our house with a recording sent by their son in Vietnam, Mike. We sat on couches around our coffee table and listened. I don't remember anything Mike said, but I remember his voice. He spoke slowly and softly but with great intensity. On edge and alert.

*

I remember seeing, from across the room, the look of anguish on Jim's face as he spoke privately and quietly to one of our high school teachers. Jim was being drafted. He was seeking conscientious objector status and was putting together his case, talking with people who would write letters for him. He was successful. He didn't have to carry a gun. I think he became a combat medic, and it was as such that he was killed. I remembered that look on his face when, years later, I found his name on the Wall.

*

Gus was a lifelong friend of my father's. He had one son and four daughters, and he bought a ranch in the northeast corner of California where he hoped he and his son Tom would run cattle someday.

I remember the day we heard that Tom had been killed in Vietnam. He was first reported "missing in action," with his death reported soon after. A soldier came to their door with the news. Tom's mother was given a sedative. I didn't see Gus's initial grief. He was a large man with a barrel chest and a wide, ruddy face. I have an image of him as a powerful animal caught in a trap.

When my father and I saw him later, Gus told us about going to an office to sign papers related to his son's death. The clerk put one paper after another in front of him, explaining the need for this or that. Gus waved his hand and said softly, "Whatever the rules are," as he signed. But when he was finished, as he rose to go, he picked up a paperweight on the counter, reared back, and threw it hard at the office wall. I don't know how much damaged this caused or what became of it. Probably nothing.

When Gus and my father were talking about Nixon going to China a few years later, Gus suddenly said bitterly, "I wish they'd make up their minds which slant-eyed-son-of-a-bitch is our friend."

But pain and anger can't be the whole story of grief. We want to find meaning in our suffering. Some of those who lost someone in Vietnam were consoled by the fall of the Berlin Wall and the end of Communism. Perhaps their loss helped bring this about. Vietnam, the Dunkirk of the Cold War, followed by victory. Maybe. But we want more. We want high ideals. Ideals as precious as life itself.

There was a party one evening at my parents' house on Depot Hill in Capitola. Gus took me out into the dark onto the lawn above the ocean. It was time for a teaching moment. As we stood alone side by side looking out into the darkness where the sea was, he began to solemnly intone:

"Fourscore and seven years ago our fathers brought forth on this continent as new nation, conceived in liberty and dedicated to the proposition that all men are created equal..."

He was reciting the Gettysburg Address.

I discreetly helped him in a couple places where he stumbled, and he got through it. "I want you to think about these words," he said, "I want you to think about what they mean and why they are important, and I don't want you to forget them." Then we went back inside.

*

I was dining alone quietly at Mac's Patio one summer evening after working at the motel, when a woman I didn't know sat down in the chair opposite me.

"I saw you and I was wondering about...if you were going to be drafted."

I told her I had a student deferment.

There was an awkward silence.

"My son was killed in Vietnam," she said.

I mumbled that I was sorry.

There was another awkward silence.

She suddenly seemed to feel she was intruding. "I just had to know that you were all right. That you were safe."

She slowly got up and walked away.

I left the money for my check, went out the door, and walked the short distance to the sea wall. The sun was still up. Mr. Lampe, a man from our neighborhood, was there with a tame racoon on a leash. A few children and their parents were gathered round, looking and smiling and asking questions. "His name is Boomer," Lampe said. After a minute or two of watching the racoon and the children, I joined the crowd on the Esplanade.

Later, I told my family about seeing the racoon.

Wasn't That a Time?

Lee Harvey Oswald was assassinated on my eleventh birthday. I don't cite this fact to advance a new conspiracy theory, but rather to place myself on the Timeline of History. *When* we are shapes *who* we are. The historian Page Smith once made this point to a group of us students at U.C. Santa Cruz, and he illustrated it by saying that the Spanish Civil War had been a formative event of his youth. Some years later he bragged about having been an early supporter of Jesse Jackson for President. I was tempted to ask him, "Just what was it about the Spanish Civil War that made you think Jesse Jackson would make a good president?" but thought better of asking such an inane question.

Political scientists have confirmed that people have a high level of impressionability between the ages of fourteen and twenty-four. My own political ideas formed themselves gradually between 1964, when I first began doing some systematic thinking, and 1974, when I was firmly ensconced within the libertarian spectrum. Johnathan Haidt has refined the data to show that Age-in-1968 predicts voting patterns for years afterwards. Indeed, 1968 was a year of war, riots and assassinations that I remember well. Certainly it provided some impetus toward my libertarianism, yet, for many of my contemporaries, it made them more likely to become Democrats. I have puzzled over this and can't explain why. Then, neither can I explain why, by the end of 1916, everyone in Europe wasn't an anarchist.

The great public event of my youth was the Vietnam war, a war made immediate by nightly television coverage of the fighting. Some of the people who voted for Johnson as the "peace candidate" were traumatized by his betrayal. I remember my Uncle Bob not wanting to talk about Johnson by the summer of '65. For my parents it presented a grim dilemma. As farmers, we felt about communists pretty much the same way Jews feel about Nazis. On the other hand, war with them meant much suffering. There seemed to be no good way out, other than to dream of hanging Lyndon Johnson after somehow cheaply halting Ho Chi Minh.

Someday I should go back and read the newspapers of the time for a better look, but my impression is that just about the only people *publicly* against the war in 1965, once regular U.S. troops were on the ground, were communists, pacifists, and my Aunt Minnie. (My maiden aunt was old enough to have formed her views in the irreverent 1920s, rather than the conformist 1930s and 40s.) Quiet opposition to the war was there from the beginning. Most poignant was that of veterans who had seen the hell of World War II and patriotically kept their mouths shut while they quietly arranged for their sons to join the National Guard or get a medical excuse from a friendly doctor. I have heard it said that in some counties in the Midwest there were no antiwar demonstrations, but the only people selected for the draft were petty criminals.

What we needed was for someone with a following and impeccable anti-communist credentials to step-up and lead opposition to the war while articulating an alternative strategy for defeating communism. But who? Senator Bob Taft, the conservative Republican who was leery of land wars in Asia, was dead. Barry Goldwater said critical things about the draft and implied during his campaign that we could win a war with air and sea power alone. Milton Friedman opposed the draft. Presumably, this meant that any war we could not fight with volunteers should not be fought at all. (By the way, we don't really have an all-volunteer army as long as the money is conscripted.) Robert Welch, the head of the anti-communist John Birch Society, called for U.S. withdrawal from Vietnam in August 1965, but he had been read out of conservatism by William Buckley and the *National Review* and out of polite society by the mainstream media, and he was afraid that his members would not back him. Ayn Rand criticized the war, but it was not her main focus, and her argument that the war was "altruistic" would have left most people scratching their heads. The Traditionalist Conservative intellectual Russell Kirk was against the war only in his private conversations. One wonders what his conversations with his magazine editor, the hawkish Buckley, were like.

*

The war was on top of the ongoing civil rights movement. When I first became aware of the civil rights movement, it seemed to be all about segregation and voting rights in the South – not something that had much impact on us in California. It first affected my family in the form of the California Fair Housing Act of 1962. This was of special interest to us because we had gone into the motel business, and the Act would require us to rent rooms to black people. My parents had no problem with this, and when the first black couple presented themselves, my father gladly rented them a room. But he grumbled that if a black person showed up with a lawyer from Sacramento, the black person would be welcome, but the lawyer would be invited to leave our property.

We were very resistant to the idea that government should determine who we hired and fired. On our farm and later at our motel, our home and our workplace were the same place. To be compelled to employ someone by the threat of a lawsuit was tantamount to being told that we had to invite someone to our home.

During the summers of 1970, '71, and '72, I was the "day manager" of our motel, and Wilma was our night manager. Wilma was white, looked like she had been born before 1920, and had the accent of a Daughter of the Old South, which meant she had grown up with segregation. I, of course, rented rooms to all races. But one morning Wilma proudly told my father and me that the night before she had lied to a black person that we had no vacancies. I guess she thought she was protecting us from becoming the local "colored accommodation." My father was not happy, but I don't know what he said to her.

I sometimes think of this incident, and it makes me sad. Was it a family that wanted the room? Did the father have to explain to his wife and children why he didn't get one?

People like Wilma were dying off, and the Federal government decided to give their death a nudge with the Civil Rights Act of 1964. This *might* have worked if it had been used as a sort of temporary "shock therapy" – getting us to non-discrimination more quickly than otherwise. Instead, it permanently institutionalized coercion and made it difficult to put race relations back on a totally voluntary basis. After all, isn't the ultimate goal to replace respect for legislation with respect for each other? Title VII of this civil rights act, the part that regulates employment and sometimes led to quotas and credentialism, should have at least had a sunset clause and expired by 1995.

In an alternative universe, in those places where public accommodations were largely segregated because of the hosts' fear of losing trade (rather than by law), an agreement among a critical mass of them to all desegregate on the same day would have suddenly shifted the burdens of fewer choices and more search time onto the backs of the racists. Town by town, as the cost of being a racist rose, any remaining segregation, and eventually racism itself, would have faded away.

In the case of segregated lunch counters, it is interesting to ponder what would have happened if the lunch counter owners could not have socialized the cost of maintaining segregation by relying on tax-supported police to enforce their preferences, especially where that preference was weak, either because the owners of the lunch counters were embarrassed by segregation or thought they could earn more money without it. (Northern-owned chain stores often fit these categories.) Private enforcement of justice selects strong property rights, but it also selects for the efficient use of property.

Because it is in the interest of employers to hire from a large pool of potential workers, employers have an incentive not to discriminate by race. Because it is in the interest of labor unions to keep the pool of potential workers small, unions have an incentive to practice racial discrimination. Granting a union monopoly bargaining rights under the National Labor Relations Act strengthened the "whites only" unions of the 1930s to the 1960s. Occupational licenses could also be used to exclude Blacks. Historically, many of the fastest rising minority groups have countered discrimination by embracing self-employment. Once these firms grow, their proprietors can earn extra profits by finding and hiring members of their group who are being undervalued by the other employers.

Where capital markets are well developed, nobody knows the race of stock and bond holders. The rights of all savers and investors are equal. As savings grow and the wealth of a group rises, it becomes more important as a source of potential customers and earns "green power," in the phrase of Adam Clayton Powell.

The civil rights revolution has not lived up to its promise. By a number of measures Blacks, as a whole, have not made as much progress as one would have expected. Yes, this *is* because they are victims of oppression. Where people are mistaken is when they attribute this oppression to racism, an understandable error, given history and the fact that there are racists out there. The truth is that we have institutions that oppress people of all races: unaccountable law enforcement and the drug war, the public schools, the banking system, labor market regulations and regulations that harass the self-employed, taxes, the welfare state, the warfare state, and more, depending on how finely you break it down. Blacks, per se, are not the target of these policies and institutions. They are collateral damage, just as many Whites are.

This should give us hope. If all Whites were irredeemably racist, cleverly designing everything to serve their racist purpose, then, in a country no more than 15 percent black, there would be nothing left for Blacks to do but ... what? Destroy their communities with symbolic gestures of rage? Try to coerce all white people into therapy and expect that to work? The fact that our rulers are "equal opportunity oppressors" means that victims of all races should work together to free themselves.

Beginning with the Watts Riot of 1965, there was a "race riot season" every summer through 1968, a phenomenon that stirred as much soul-searching as the war. Blacks in America face the problem that they did not win their civil rights until after the door of economic opportunity through free markets had begun closing. Add to this the fact that our cities are ruled by unresponsive political patronage machines, and the odds against Black progress become difficult to surmount. In response to the riots, the powerful followed their usual strategy of throwing money in the direction of the discontented, hoping it would keep them quiet – money filtered through "leaders" who became adjuncts of the machine and manage the black vote.

Liberty is the opposite of slavery. A slave is owned by another. A free man owns himself. A slave is forced to associate with his owner. A free man chooses his associates. *In a totally free society, all relationships are voluntary.* This is the point where the opponents of liberty mount their attack by claiming that *in a free society racism will run rampant.* In their view, we need a big state to extirpate racism.

There are reasons to doubt this claim. First, for most of American history the state was used to prop up racism. Second, if racism is so ubiquitous, how do we get a majority to elect a nonracist government? Some antiracists propose to solve this problem by putting us all under the tutelage of a self-anointed enlightened elite, who will not only control our behavior, but will attempt to divine and craft our thoughts as well. (And of course, some day they will declare victory and relinquish this power!)

We need an alternative vision: Radical freedom of association. With throughgoing free markets and as much political decentralization as possible, the racists would be bypassed, infiltrated, surrounded, isolated, inundated, overwhelmed, and routed! And this would be accomplished with a minimum of rancor.

*

The riots of the 1960s weren't only about race; they were partly a response to the mounting casualties of the war.

During the summer I was fifteen, Martin Luther King Jr. and Robert Kennedy were assassinated.

*

Spring 1970. We senior boys at Soquel High School were excused from class and brought together for an assembly in the cafeteria to hear the military recruiters make their pitches. The first recruiter to speak was from the Air Force. He talked a lot about the educational opportunities the Air Force had to offer, both while in service and as college aid afterwards. The Navy recruiter was next. He made the same pitch. He had a long list of the career specialties you could apply for when you enlisted. Then the Marine Corps recruiter stood up. He looked us over for a moment and announced, "I'm a Marine! We kill people!" A raucous cheer filled the room. No, we weren't eager to kill anyone. We were cheering his brutal honesty. He clearly knew that his only hope for recruits was to segment the market and earn the respect of the few who might be open to him. I know of two from our class who joined the Marines. They survived Vietnam, though one of them was wounded. Years later he said to me, "I was shot," in a surprised tone.

I knew I wasn't going to join the Marines. Probably, at age eighteen, if it looked like I was about to be drafted, I would have joined the Navy. But this had its risks. You might end up in Hawaii or cruising the Mediterranean, but you could also end up in the Mekong Delta like John Kerry. One person I knew who joined the Navy came under fire when his ship attacked Haiphong harbor. There was another person I knew who, when he received his army draft notice in the mail, immediately went to a neighboring state and joined the Air Force. He drew the dangerous assignment of flying in and out of Khe Sanh while it was surrounded and under siege. He survived the war, but was deathly ill for a time with Agent Orange poisoning. Agent Orange was a defoliant the Air Force used to remove the leaves from trees and reveal enemy trails in the jungle.

I was twelve years old when Vietnam went from being an "advisors' war" to being a war of regular troops and bombing runs. My thoughts at the time were: "Communism is evil, and we will beat them fairly quickly." I was fifteen years old when the Tet offensive happened. My thoughts were: "Communism is evil, but fighting it causes us to do evil things too." I was seventeen years old when Kent State happened. My thought was "Can any good be salvaged from this?" Unfortunately, I spent too much time reading the columnist Joe Alsop and Time Magazine simply because these were readily available, and both of them were notoriously over optimistic about the progress of Vietnamization and the advisability of gradual withdrawal.

Four students were killed at Kent State University in May 1970 during an antiwar protest when National Guard troops fired on them. I remember feeling angry when I heard about this, without having a clear idea who I was angry with. I think it was the sheer stupidity of it all that got to me. The real antiwar action was in draft resistance, tax resistance (there was some), insubordination among the troops, and the restive electorate. A confrontation between college students and soldiers in a cloud of tear gas was *theater*, and no one is supposed to die in a theatrical performance. The play being enacted was a conflict of generations, Boomers plaintively asking their parents, "How could you send us to war? You built Disneyland for us, for heaven's sake." After Kent State, I stopped watching television news.

Most of my friends and I applied for college student deferments when we graduated from high school. One school friend a grade younger than me avoided the draft by fleeing to Canada. In later years, I got to know someone who went "underground" to avoid the draft.

By and large, the Vietnam generation was made up of the children of the World War Two generation. The sons' experience resonated with that of the fathers', sometimes creating conflict (known as the "generation gap") and sometimes creating closeness. There were earnest discussions going on about what we owe to humanity, political majorities, our country, and the government, and what that duty requires. Combine this with the contemporary civil disobedience strategy of Martin Luther King Jr. and the civil rights movement, and you can understand why the question, "Why should the law be obeyed?" was the preeminent philosophical question of my youth.

That question became an obsession of mine, framed variously as Majority Rule versus Minority Rights, or Democracy versus Liberty, or Dependence on Government versus Independence from it. Once I discovered the Libertarian tradition, all became clear. I joined those thinkers from Lord Acton to Robert Nozick who proclaim liberty to be, not the Highest End of Man (something on which there will always be fundamental disagreement), but the highest *political* end.

This tradition is virtually invisible to students in the government schools (of course!), but it is powerfully presented by a number of authors I can recommend. The classic work, and the one likely to be most familiar, is *On Civil Disobedience* (1849) by Henry David Thoreau. Thoreau was moved by his disgust with government support of slavery and the Mexican War to refuse to pay a tax. The only immediate result of this was that he spent a night in Concord's jail, but the essay he wrote about his experience later influenced Gandhi and Martin Luther King, Jr. Thoreau's argument is based on the claims of conscience and the insight that, if everyone heeded those claims, injustice would cease.

More systematic in his approach was the nineteenth century British philosopher Herbert Spencer, who wrote the essay "The Right to Ignore the State" (1844.) Spencer, a descendant of dissenting Protestants, began with his opposition to being taxed to support the established Church of England. He ended by concluding that no person should be hindered from peacefully pursuing any purpose he or she chooses. While Thoreau was, at least potentially, a revolutionary, Spencer was an evolutionist.

He imagined that initially only a small number of people would withdraw from the state, and that that number would grow at a gradual pace that allowed voluntary institutions to smoothly take up the legitimate tasks of cooperative action.

In 1870 American lawyer Lysander Spooner published *No Treason: The Constitution of No Authority*. Spooner was a radical abolitionist who opposed making war on the southern secessionists. He saw no inconsistency in this. States, he said, have the right to secede from the union, and slaves have the right to secede from their masters. We should work to free the slaves by direct action, rather than through the medium of the state. Using legal arguments, Spooner took great pains to show that the U.S. Constitution is not a legal contract and that it confers no authority on anyone.

Moving forward 100 years, we come to *In Defense of Anarchism* (1970) by Robert Paul Wolff. Following Kant, Wolff says that we cannot be said to be making a moral decision when that decision is influenced by the threat of coercion. Moral choices must be free choices. To surrender our autonomy, to "outsource" our moral judgement to the state, is to surrender our humanity --even deny our humanity. Wolff's stirring conclusion is, "For the autonomous man, there is no such thing, strictly speaking, as a *command*."

The same ground is covered in a very accessible manner by Michael Huemer in *The Problem of Political Authority: An Examination of the Right to Coerce and the Duty to Obey* (2013). Huemer is an intuitionist. Much of his argument advances by analogy. Huemer will have you nodding your head in agreement with what seems to be obvious. He then draws out the radical implications of that agreement until you find yourself agreeing that there is no political authority. But Huemer does much more. He writes engagingly and persuasively about psychology, public choice, the prospects for anarchism and more. If I were to make a list of three or four books to recommend to anyone willing to make a serious study of libertarianism, this book of Huemer's would be on the list.

*

The average person will tell you that we live in a Democracy and "Democracy confers Authority." I find this line of reasoning distressing. The first vote I ever cast, for Richard Nixon, was stupid. For the next fifty years, except for a couple Capitola City Council members, *every candidate I have ever voted for for any office has lost.* That's one act of stupidity followed by half a century of futile gestures. And then people tell me that my "participation in the democratic process" has somehow sanctified the crimes of the people elected. People worry about whether votes are counted accurately. They should reflect on voting's role in legitimizing the arrogant assertion of power by whoever wins the count.

*

Students at a Christian High School told me that our purpose on earth is to fulfill the Will of God. Someone else told me that our highest calling it to be guided by our reason. Some say we are here to serve humanity, defined as everyone on earth. Others say that we can only truly love the people we know and see face to face. Some widen the circle of our concern to include animals. People come naturally to the idea that we have duties we owe to others. It is at the foundation of our humanity and of civilization.

But what do we owe *the state*?

Nothing.

Mentors

When it comes to politics, I'm sometimes chided for my obvious stupidity and ignorance, often coupled with the charge that I have allied myself with yahoos. My friends might tepidly agree with me on foreign policy, listen politely as I present the case for free trade, or puzzle over my thoughts on banking and the monetary system, but when I venture to denounce Roosevelt's New Deal and Johnson's Great Society, stunned silence is usually the best reaction I can hope for. From my earliest youth I could see that Social Democracy is just a means of dominating people, but I needed arguments to back up this insight. Where could I find them?

So, at a tender age I embarked on a life-long quest *to find intelligent opposition to big government.* The problem was that I had no mentors. My parents voted Republican, but they didn't care a hoot about the Republican Party or spend any time discussing its platform. They just knew in their bones that the Democratic Party was the party of "tax, spend, and elect," in the supposed words of Roosevelt's advisor Harry Hopkins, and that this approach would ultimately destroy the country. My parents were thorough readers of newspapers and magazines, and they encouraged their children to read books, but they didn't have the patience to read books themselves. There was no list of titles they could point me toward. There was no tattered copy of John Flynn's *The Roosevelt Myth* or Henry Hazlitt's *Economics in One Lesson* on a shelf at home where I could take it down and get started.

When I began, William Buckley was the most celebrated conservative in America. No one could deny that *he* was intelligent. He used big words and Latin phrases, and the precise words he needed came easily to his lips in an upperclass Northeastern accent. He was also everywhere. His column was in the paper, he had a weekly program on PBS, and the magazine he edited, *The National Review*, was available in my high school library. Here was someone the left could not dismiss. Here was a place for me to get started. So, I began to read and listen to Buckley.

But Buckley's writings didn't provide much sustenance. Much of it centered on the partisan squabbling of the day. The rest focused on our confrontation with communism or made vague (to me) references to Catholic doctrine. I wanted to set aside the issues of the day and get down to studying the nitty gritty of how society worked, but Buckley didn't provide that, and I lost interest in him.

Economics looked like the place to renew my search so, in the summer of 1968, I went to the public library, found the economics shelf, and checked out every book that looked understandable. One book, *Man, Money, and Goods* by John Gambs, proved to be a useful primer on supply and demand. The others, by Keynesians George Soule, Stuart Chase, John Kenneth Galbraith, and Robert Heilbroner, were no help at all. (Heilbroner's *The Worldly Philosophers*, at least, was interesting.) I remember that one of these authors briefly referred to Friedrich Hayek (this is the first time I heard Hayek's name) saying that the thesis of *The Road to Serfdom* had been refuted by Professor So-and-So. I was so naïve, I remember saying to myself, "Well, I guess that means I don't have to waste time with Hayek."

After this disappointing foray into economics, the Book-of-the-Month Club caught my eye. This was a club in which a panel of successful authors and critics selected a book each month that they recommended. Sort of like Oprah today. They would sell you that book, or let you select an alternate from their catalogue, or let you skip making a purchase that month. Intellectuals looked down on the club as providing "middlebrow" literature to aspirational members of the middle class, particularly those who had not gone to college. (Back then, lots of middle class people had not gone to college.) In those days before the Internet, the club also attracted people who lived in rural areas where there were no bookstores.

All I cared about was this: if I joined the club for a year, I could receive, *for free*, all ten volumes (volume eleven hadn't been written yet) of Will and Ariel Durant's *The Story of Civilization* along with Will Durant's *The Story of Philosophy*. This was as I was starting my junior year of high school.

My approach to high school was this: My outside reading came first, then the English and History classes claimed my attention, followed by Speech and Debate and Journalism. In math, Spanish, and Chemistry I usually did the bare minimum I needed to pass. In truth, I found these last three subjects difficult and boring, and I probably would have needed one-on-one instruction to do well in them, something high school was not set up to provide. My grades were barely adequate to get into U.C. Santa Cruz (more selective in those days), but my English and history SATs and the points I got for graduating from a local high school put me over the top.

I decided to read the Durant books, along with another volume of his, *The Pleasures of Philosophy*, by high school graduation, with occasional breaks to read a novel. The problem is that this delayed my libertarian education for a few years. Durant's work, which is actually a history of Europe to the French Revolution, contained no economics, no economic history, and no history of social institutions or law. The great theme of his work is Faith versus Reason, and he focuses on art, literature, philosophy, and the doings of kings. The subtext of his work is a reverence for High Culture. Interesting stuff, but the social sciences don't intrude on his narrative, thus reading him delayed my project of understanding how society works.

Still, Durant's philosophy books captured my imagination, and I began to read and try to puzzle out Plato, Descartes, Spinoza, Voltaire, and James during the summer after high school, vowing to major in philosophy in college, where I would have teachers to help me. There was another attraction to philosophy: with the country tearing itself apart over the war and racial violence, thinking about metaphysics and epistemology was like taking soma.

By the end of 1971 at UCSC, I was ready to revisit economics, so I signed up for the introductory course taught by Jacob Michaelsen. Michaelsen was the most free-market professor in the department. He said this was because he had spent a decade listening to Milton Friedman. This was literally true. Michaelsen started at the University of Chicago as a freshman and stayed there through his PhD. Naturally, we read *Capitalism and Freedom* and were given the Chicago "take" on economic subjects, including criticism of Nixon's New Economic Policy speech of the previous summer that established price controls and broke the last link between the dollar and gold. We were also exposed to a critique of some of Presidential Candidate George McGovern's economic positions.

I had two big take-aways from this class. The first is that, in Friedman's words, "Inflation is always and everywhere a monetary phenomenon." Which means that *inflation is a deliberate policy* engineered by the political class and the Central Bank. Which means that when most politicians and media figures talk about inflation *they are lying, or at least evading telling the truth.* You don't need to be a conspiracy theorist to recognize propaganda and connect it to its evil purpose.

The second take-away from the class was this: Some writers assume a totalitarian state as the "default option" for society and then grudgingly concede some role for the market. Michaelsen started with a pure free market, and then reluctantly conceded certain tasks to the government. Now, as a Chicago economist, Michaelsen ended up with a sizable amount of government, but the fact that he started with anarchy as his premise introduced a novel way of looking at things.

We also read a short book critiquing anarcho-communism, *The Political Economy of the New Left*, by Assar Lindbeck. Lindbeck's main point is that, for all but the simplest economic relationships, markets and bureaucracy are our only alternative ways of organizing society. Lindbeck's book is the place where I first saw Murray Rothbard's name. In passing, Lindbeck calls Rothbard that rare member of the New Left who embraces markets. I didn't pick up on this reference.

Mentors II

One of the advantages of the old fashioned bookstore is that you can browse through the shelves and find books you never knew you wanted. I found *Indispensable Enemies: The Politics of Misrule in America* by Walter Karp among the drug paraphernalia, posters, and incense in the book section of a head shop. Karp was an outstandingly eloquent writer. This book on American history and institutions is the best sustained attack on Marx's class theory I have ever read, and he does it without mentioning Marx. When I finished reading Karp's book, I immediately began reading it a second time, caught in the excitement of finding something wonderful.

No man ever forgets his first love or his first bookstore. My first bookstore was the legendary Hip Pocket Books on Pacific Avenue in Santa Cruz in the mid-1960s. The place was casual and noncommercial and had lots of paperbacks. Two life-sized bronze nudes, one man and one woman, were mounted outside above the awning. A small coffee house called the Catalyst was in the back. The whole enterprise looked like it had wandered down the coast from North Beach in San Francisco just as the Beats were being supplanted by the Hippies. I found Orwell's *Animal Farm* and *1984* there, and the unexpected treasure I found was a copy of Orwell's *Essays*.

The Hip Pocket was sold after a few years, and its descendant is Bookshop Santa Cruz. This is where I was browsing in the spring of 1974 when I came upon a copy of *The Machinery of Freedom* by David Friedman. Here was a free market book among the usual abundance of socialist screeds on the shelf. I bought it and devoured it. That quarter, my last at UCSC, I had signed up for a class in the History of Economic Thought taught by Peter Gottschalk. Gottschalk had put Hayek's *The Road to Serfdom* on the reading list, so when I saw it on the shelf along with a book of Hayek's essays, I bought these too.

By the time I finished reading these three books, I was calling myself a libertarian. David Friedman (who turned out to be Milton Friedman's son) pushed out the free market frontier considerably. Not only that, but his sharp distinction between voluntary action and coercion made it possible to apply a universal principle to conflicts. Hayek's critique of collectivist solutions was a further argument for voluntary relationships. Hayek connected me with the long liberal tradition, while David Friedman was a link to an exciting new movement.

It wasn't long before I was bringing my new insights to Gottschalk's small discussion class. One of the books Gottschalk assigned was *Social Perspectives in the History of Economic Thought* by Everett Burtt Jr. This book, surprisingly, has an entire chapter on the Austrian School. Peter Gottschalk was a socialist, but once he realized that I was a budding free market person, he suggested that I look into the Austrians. He, of course, would have liked to convert me to socialism, but once he saw that this was not possible, his attitude was, "If you're going to go free market, I want you to read the best free market people," by which he meant Mises and Company. Not only that, but Gottschalk invited Dave Merrick from the local Libertarian Party group to speak to the class. It may be difficult for today's students to grasp this, but back in those days the professors possessed intellectual integrity and were eager to provide students with the strongest arguments against what the professor himself believed.

I don't remember exactly what Dave Merrick said to us when he spoke, but he made a strong impression on me. First, he was not simply free-market; he was *breathtakingly* free market, following David Friedman in talking about having police, the courts, and even law itself provided by the market, in other words, provided by voluntary cooperation alone. Secondly, he was not simply anti-war, he was *breathtakingly* anti-war, questioning all U.S. military involvement abroad and even the desirability of having a standing army. But the thing that impressed me the most was the *combination* of these two viewpoints.

The Cold War was more than a quarter century old at the time. People of my generation had grown up viewing free market people as the ones most eager to take a stand against Communism abroad and support large military budgets. This seemed natural because communists want to abolish markets. I was soon to learn that this combination of free markets and militarism was an historical anomaly. Classical liberalism had been born in opposition to standing armies and taxes for war. I soon began my years of sampling its rich literature, from Locke and the Levelers in the 17th Century to Trenchard and Gordon, Jefferson, Paine and Smith in the 18th century, to Cobden and Bright, Constant, Bastiat, Acton, Spencer, Sumner, and Auberon Herbert in the 19th century, and on up to Garet Garrett, John Flynn, Albert J. Nock, Isabell Paterson and Frank Chodorov in 1930s to 1950s America. (Along, of course, with Mises and Hayek.) I also came to see that opposition to government intervention at home and opposition to government intervention abroad reinforce each other. Peace and liberty are natural allies.

Philosophy had taught me to look for a universal ethics – moral principles that apply to all human beings. This search comes to grief on the brute fact that agents of the state are placed outside the moral universe. An individual person was not to lie, steal, kidnap, counterfeit, or kill. But, clothed in the alleged authority of the state, one could do these things as long as they are called elections, taxation, conscription, monetary policy and war. Libertarianism appealed to me because it is simply morality applied to everyone: "Equal rights for all and special privileges for none" in the only coherent sense of "equality," "rights,'" and "privilege."

By that fall, I was in the Santa Clara University library setting aside my study of debits and credits to drag out old magazines and read Karl Hess's "The Death of Politics" and Murray Rothbard's "Confessions of A Right Wing Liberal." Even today I cannot reread these, along with Rothbard's "Left and Right" and Leonard Liggio's "Why the Futile Crusade?" without emotion. I felt relief and gratitude; finally, the political world made sense. And I also felt some anger; why are these ideas kept from us? We are the presumptive heirs of the great classical liberal/libertarian tradition that weaves through and redeems Western Civilization. But who teaches this tradition to each generation? Not the political parties, not the media, not the schools. We don't know our mother and father.

*

It was now time to make a serious study of economics, focusing on Mises, Hayek and Rothbard. One day I walked into the business school library and noticed a pile of books in a trash can. I asked the attendant about then, and she said they were "discards" and that I could have any of them. So, I reached into the stack and pulled out the two-volume Volker Fund first edition of Rothbard's *Man, Economy and State*. "You're throwing out Rothbard?" "Yes" she responded, "We have two copies." Sure enough, Volker had sent Santa Clara two copies, and the school kept one on the shelf, while I took the discard off their hands. Now, where to get Mises's *Human Action*? I learned that Karen

Huffman and her husband were selling Mises's books out of their garage in Mountain View. So, I drove to their quiet residential street and bought *Human Action* and a couple of other books. Getting books from the trash and from a garage "bookstore" reinforced the romantic idea that I had joined some sort of clandestine, underground movement. Hence, I was pleasantly surprised when Hayek won his Nobel Prize in economics soon after.

By May 1974, I was going to Libertarian Party meetings in Santa Cruz. These might be attended by six to eight people and always ended at a late-night restaurant, where there was a lot of conversation and laughter. We circulated petitions to get our candidates on the ballot, sent speakers to high school classes, wrote letters to the editor, had literature tables at events, and things like that. I met some really bizarre people during this time, but I won't go into that. Hey, it was Santa Cruz ....it was the Seventies......it was the Libertarian Party.......

As long as Dave Merrick, a man of integrity and intelligence who was, well, normal, was involved, I would stay involved too. Things brightened even more when Richard Ebeling began coming to our meetings. Ebeling was in the Bay Area at the Institute for Humane Studies and had either recently received his PhD in economics or was close to doing so. Ebeling had started his intellectual journey with Ayn Rand, gone on to discover the Foundation for Economic Education, and then became an Austrian with the goal of becoming an academic economist.

Back in those days, almost every libertarian you met had come from Rand and continued to love her novels. Some of our meetings ended up being Ayn Rand trivia nights, as members tried to stump each other with details from her books. I didn't take part. I'd never read any of Rand's novels. Still haven't, mainly because once I had read a couple of her nonfiction books, I didn't see the need to go beyond that.

Why was Rand such an influence? Well, fiction goes down easy, and there were so few other people advancing radical individualism at the time. I think, too, that for many young people, Rand was both the first philosopher they ever read *and* the first libertarian they ever read. Either of these two experiences by itself can be exciting for a young person, so Rand was doubly exciting. I, on the other hand, had never heard of Rand until after I had a degree in philosophy and after I had become a libertarian. For me, she was one more writer to coolly appraise.

By this time, Ebeling shared Rothbard's irreverent attitude toward Rand, and he would entertain us with his wicked Rand imitation:

[Ayn to Nathaniel: "I am ze most rational voman is ze world! You are ze most rational man! Ve must make loff!]

More seriously, Ebeling came to one of our meetings to report on his attendance at the now legendary South Royalton Conference, which rejuvenated Austrian free-market economics. He gave us a sense of a movement on the move, something that addressed the needs of our time and our society, and something that was attracting bright young scholars. He was also proud that when Milton Friedman unexpectedly showed up at the conference, he had had the courage to publicly ask the famous Chicago economist a barbed question.

Ebeling arranged for Dave Merrick and me to visit Antony Sutton at Sutton's home in Aptos. Sutton was an English-born scholar who had been fired by the Hoover Institution at Stanford. Sutton's field was Western technology and Soviet economic development. After writing a scholarly work on this subject, he followed it with a popular book called *National*

Suicide, on how the West transferred its technology to the Soviet Union and, in effect, kept the Cold War going and indirectly subsidized North Vietnam. Sutton sought publicity. He testified at the 1972 Republican Convention on his work. This made Sutton too hot for Hoover to handle, so he was pushed out and became an independent scholar.

When Dave and I met Sutton, he had finished his book *Wall Street and the Bolshevik Revolution* and was working on *Wall Street and FDR*. The first book made the case that Western banks had helped the Bolsheviks consolidate power. The FDR book was about Roosevelt's career before he ran for office, when he had been a bagman for the New York political machine (using that mainstay of honest graft, an insurance agency) and had promoted some dubious investment schemes.

What I remember from our meeting is that Sutton showed us a framed specimen he had mounted on the wall of a currency that had become worthless. (Chiang Kai Shek's, I think.) He spoke of his admiration for Richard Cobden, the 19th century English free-trader who had opposed war and imperialism, recommending that we read Cobden's essay "How Wars Are Got Up in India." He also said that Britain made a big mistake when it entered World War I. Britain should have heeded Cobden's warning not to enter into a "balance of power" alliance. Finally, Sutton spoke warmly of the "Greens," by which he meant the libertarians who had opposed both the Reds and the Whites in the Russian Civil War. As we left, he gave us each a copy of his Bolshevik Revolution book.

I saw Sutton one more time when he came to my house to give an informal talk to a group of people who were interested in libertarianism. I don't recall seeing him again after that. His life became sad. He went from being published by the Hoover Institution, to being published by the respected conservative publisher, Arlington House, to being published by small presses, the only ones that would touch him as his work went further from the mainstream. His marriage ended. In spite of all this, he continued to work, and his work continues to be cited by people doing power-elite analysis.

*

Through the years I have attended many libertarian conferences and conventions for the opportunity they afford to hear my favorite authors speak in person. Here are some brief impressions: Murray Rothbard was always enthusiastic, irreverent, profound and *funny*. (See for yourself by viewing his talks preserved at mises.org.) Thomas Sowell has said, "I don't have *faith* in the market. I have *evidence* about the market." And when he spoke he backed up everything he said with statistics. Walter Williams was both likeable and logical. I came away from hearing David Friedman, who has his PhD. in physics and is a professor of Law and Economics, thinking "This guy must have the highest IQ of anyone I've ever seen." The historian Ralph Raico combined history and ideas in a compelling manner, drawing liberalism's lessons from events. Raico always suggested further reading as he spoke, and the list I compiled from him alone was enough for a liberal education.

Leonard Liggio, the historian who seemed to know everything and everyone, impressed me a lot. Liggio's expertise was in foreign policy. When he was the head of the Institute for Humane Studies and IHS was in Menlo Park, California I drove up there a couple times to hear speakers, and two or three times he brought whoever happened to be their current resident scholar to Santa Cruz to speak.

Liggio's opposition to war and intervention in the affairs of other nations was informed by his deep knowledge of how societies work. He didn't have much fear of communism. Ludwig von Mises had shown that socialism, by destroying market prices, makes it impossible to allocate capital in productive ways. As a result, socialist economies are doomed to collapse. The more territory the communists controlled, the sooner this would become apparent. According to Liggio, the best way to defeat communism would be to ignore it and embrace free markets at home. Vietnam abandoned communist economics as unworkable eleven years after the war ended, confirming Liggio's wisdom.

*

Liggio was also informed by the insights of Herbert Spencer, the 19th century British philosopher and one of the founders of sociology. Spencer contrasted two types of societies: The "Military" and the "Industrial." In a military society, everyone is forced to work to achieve goals determined by the state. In an industrial society, people are free to do what they want, so there are as many life plans as there are people. People in an industrial society further their plans by engaging in voluntary cooperation. This voluntary cooperation generates both civil society and market prices.

A society organized from the top with chains of command and coercive status relationships is a society organized for war, and it can easily be turned to that purpose, while a society that organizes itself voluntarily with individual rights and contracts is a society organized for peace. Moreover, nations organized on the voluntary principle are more likely to cooperate peacefully with one another, produce abundantly, create technological innovations, and attract the allegiance of good people. In Spencer's terms, the freest are the fittest, so war and tyranny will eventually die out. It is only the continuous application of force and propaganda by ruling elites that prevents this desirable outcome.

*

I looked forward to my opportunity to hear Karl Hess speak. Hess was much beloved in the libertarian community. He had been homeschooled back when virtually no one did that. (Karl's mother enrolled him in school "A" and filed a transfer to school "B." Then she enrolled Karl in school "B" and filed a transfer to school "A." The bureaucracy never realized he was gone.) Hess had been a speechwriter for Barry Goldwater. ("Extremism in the defense of liberty is no vice. Moderation in the pursuit of justice is no virtue," may not have been Hess's line, but it reflected his spirit.) His independent spirit and his passionate opposition to war and the military draft led him to anarchism, where he bounced between Rothbard and Kropotkin, while giving much attention to the nuts-and-bolts of producing stateless, self-sufficient communities. An Oscar-winning documentary film was made about him, and his book, *Dear America*, is worth reading.

The room where Hess was to speak at a libertarian conference I attended was filled to standing room in eager anticipation. The topic of his talk was "Abraham Lincoln." Hess rose in silence, all eyes on him, and solemnly announced, "Lincoln was an asshole." Half the audience was stunned speechless and most of the rest laughed nervously. Minds, I think, wandered for the rest of his talk, and I don't remember what he said. In any case, you can get a concise and polite presentation of the case against Lincoln from Thomas DiLorenzo's books.

I attended the famous debate between DiLorenzo and Harry Jaffa that took place at the Independent Institute in Oakland in 2002 on the question, "Was Lincoln the Best or the Worst President?" (Jaffa, best. DiLorenzo, worst.) Jaffa was a noted Straussian, (a follower of the philosopher Leo Strauss.) All I know about Strauss is that he was a big-government guy who believed it is OK to lie for the greater good. The neocons who led us into wars in the Middle East are allegedly his disciples. As is usual in these cases, followers split into camps. I don't recall whether Jaffa was an East Coast Straussian or a West Coast Straussian or why it matters.

Karl Hess eventually began earning his living as a welder. He would say, "If you want your neighbors to listen to you, first make sure your welds hold," so there was wisdom there to go along with his flair for drama.

I regret missing the opportunity I had to hear Friedrich Hayek speak. Probably I'll regret the day I missed Robert Higgs. I know I'm sorry I missed a chance I had to see Aaron Copeland conduct an orchestra. Copeland supported the Communist Party ticket in the 1936 election, but he was a fine composer. Politics isn't everything.

Business

Soon after I got into the auto parts business, I realized that there are two kinds of people in the world: people who pay their auto parts bill and people who don't. People who pay are found among all races, ethnicities, and genders. People who don't pay are found among all races, ethnicities and genders. If you own a small business in a competitive industry and you do anything but judge each person, employee or customer, as anything but an individual with a unique character, you are going to go out of business, or at least leave money on the table.

This imperative to judge people as individuals in a free marketplace dovetails with a legal system grounded on individual rights and our responsibility to respect each person. But before I get too philosophical, I should explain how I got from philosophy to business.

U.C. Santa Cruz was a good place to study philosophy in 1970. It was a small school in the redwoods with no grades, no football team, and no fraternities. The only major offered connected with employment was Computer Science. Few of us worried about getting a job, but by the end of my junior year I began to think about what I would do next. Graduate school in philosophy was out. To become a philosophy teacher would mean spending my entire life in school, which was not an attractive prospect. (Bryan Caplan, who became a professor, figures he is now in 47th grade.) While my department certified me as being an above average student, that was not good enough for grad school. Only the absolute cream of the crop should become professional philosophers. Michael Huemer says you should become a professional philosopher only if you feel a compulsion to spend all your waking hours thinking up arguments. Law school also was out. It takes three years. It is either boring (estates, trusts, incorporations, etc.) or adversarial (trials, divorces.) Too many people go to Law School because they don't know what else to do, and the burnouts become high school government teachers or run for office.

My family had always owned a business, and I figured business skills would have a wide application, so business suggested itself. I went to the stacks in the library (this was pre-internet) to look for a place where I could get a second major in business. I discovered I could go to Santa Clara University for two years and get an M.B.A. This seemed more impressive than a second major, and it wasn't very expensive at the time, so that is what I did.

The Santa Clara program was not at the level of Harvard, Stanford or Wharton, programs that teach you to be the CEO of a large corporation. Most of my fellow students had been working in the business world for a few years and were preparing for the promotion that would move them one step up the ladder. All classes were conveniently in the late afternoon or evening.

With my only experience being working for my family, and the airy undergraduate major of philosophy, I decided I needed to concentrate on accounting, something more solid than management or marketing. This was not such a wrenching change as it might appear. Philosophy and accounting are both highly logical, and both accounting and metaphysics seek to uncover the reality that lies behind appearances.

As a student, I was better at philosophy than at business, but I got through it without much trouble and now had to confront the question of what to do next. The most sought-after jobs were with the "Big Eight" auditing firms, so I interviewed with a couple of their reps when they visited our campus. One of these reps asked me about philosophy (He, it turns out, was interested in it too!), so most of the interview was spent talking about that. When we were finished, he confided that they were only hiring straight-A students that year, and he was talking to others like me just to kill time.

What to do? Take the CPA exam and do tax returns for people? Or, worse yet, work for the IRS? (Their rep visited our campus with a group of other speakers. During the wine-and-cheese I asked him the philosophical question of how taxation differed from robbery.)

The best alternative seemed to be to work in the accounting office of a business, preferably one in the Santa Cruz-Monterey area. Banks were on my list, and my father encouraged me to apply at County Bank of Santa Cruz, a small local bank that had been in existence for over a hundred years and all of whose twelve branches were in Santa Cruz County. When I walked in for the interview and told them I had graduated in philosophy from UCSC, the interviewer prepared to show me the door. Then I pulled out my Santa Clara MBA and told them I was a local and was immediately hired. It was that easy. I was sent to the next door office of a vice president, who welcomed me aboard and told me "A bank is a giant accounting sausage grinder!"

After six months of working as a teller and doing other tasks in some of the branches and taking a required class at Cabrillo College called "Principles of Bank Operations," I was given my own cubicle in the seven-person accounting office on the first floor of the headquarters building. That was 1976, and I earned $735 a month.

I took over the file on equipment the bank had bought and leased to customers, I worked on the new cost accounting system the bank was trying to create (cost accounting for banks was considered the next big thing), I alerted the computer people to any errors I found in the output of one of their programs, and I prepared charts and graphs on deposits for our chairman, but mostly I did payroll taxes – not the bank's payroll, but customers' payrolls. In those days, only large businesses had computers. Since we had a computer, we were in the business of doing computerized payrolls for some of our business depositors. My job was to make the correct monthly tax deposits for these customers and do their quarterly payroll tax returns. The long printouts I received listing employees and their state and federal income tax and payroll tax deductions were a revelation. Silent, automated, and routine, these represented *a vast transfer of power to a small number of people in Washington and Sacramento.*

A few months before, when I had worked at a Felton branch of the bank, I used to go to a little sandwich shop nearby for lunch. The proprietor himself carefully made each sandwich, and I remember that each sandwich came with half a banana sliced diagonally to make the customer feel he was getting something extra. One day the order came down from the IRS that I was to seize money from this sandwich guy's account and put it in the treasury's account, which, after some grumbling to my supervisor, I did.

I'm used to going to the supermarket and buying chicken parts wrapped in plastic, but I remember the time I watched my father chop the heads off a couple chickens, and we plucked them as we sat under a walnut tree on my grandfather's ranch. Just as we no longer kill our own chickens and don't have to think about doing so, so has taxation largely become sanitized and removed from the categories of predator and prey. It was much starker in earlier times, when the excise man might show up at your farm to seize your cow, or board your ship and seize your cargo, or come to your shop and seize your tools.

I was charged with one more task at the bank. I prepared the bank's sales tax returns. The bank sold coin banks, and every now and then someone would buy one for a grandchild. The trickle of money this produced for the state was about the same as the cost of my reporting it.

After two years, I left the bank to go into auto parts. On my last day, I considered putting an entry through the work that would write-off the bank's portfolio of US Treasury Securities as a bad debt, but thought better of it.

A small, community bank had been a good place to work, and the knowledge I gained doing payroll and sales tax returns served me in good stead in my next role. My father and brother had gotten into the auto parts business while I was at the bank. For a while, I worked at the bank during the week and helped in the auto parts office on Saturdays, but by July 1978 there was enough work for me to make the switch and become a full partner in Mid-County Auto Supply. Mid-County was a single location family business a little larger than a "mom and pop." We had a 5,000 square-foot building and, when we were cranking, it was me, my brother, four counter sales people, a machinist, an outside salesman, and two delivery drivers.

*

Proprietors, entrepreneurs and the self-employed in general once constituted a large percentage of the workforce. The tacit knowledge and folk wisdom this group possesses about how society works, or doesn't work, is a key ingredient in a healthy society. When that knowledge is lost, society suffers.

Some years ago, I went to a wine-and-cheese gathering for UCSC alumni. The standard "What do you do?" question led to a conversation with a fellow business owner. We bonded quickly and talked about some of our experiences. Eventually the conversation came around to this point: When it comes to understanding healthy social cooperation, *academics and their colleagues in the bureaucracy just don't get it.* Shortly thereafter, we paused to listen to a professor and a few others who were nearby talk about the state of the nation, and my new acquaintance and I just looked at each other knowingly and shook our heads.

So, what don't they get? They don't really get *markets and voluntary cooperation.* They may understand them intellectually, but they don't have a visceral feel for them. Here are some of the things my brother and I learned running our auto parts store:

Competition is real, and it doesn't let up. We sold auto parts to installers: repair shops, fleets, and do-it-yourselfers. These installers wanted the correct part. They wanted it not to be defective. They wanted it fast, and they wanted it at a low price. Professional mechanics, who made up the bulk of our business, were especially insistent on these points. If the car or truck is up on his rack ready to be worked on and the part doesn't work or arrive quickly, we would hear about it. With five other auto parts stores within a six-mile radius, losing sales was easy if you screwed up. Moreover, the traditional chain of distribution for major lines was from manufacturer to warehouse to jobber to installer. But the manufacturers are always alert for opportunities to sell direct to the jobbers, and the warehouses are always alert for opportunities to sell direct to the installers, blurring the distinctions and multiplying the number of potential competitors.

Many of the professional installers kept the local parts suppliers on their toes by having a primary supplier, from whom they bought most of their parts, and a secondary supplier they used now and then. It was an easy matter at the end of the day for a customer to look over the invoices to compare prices and see which store was giving him the best deal on each line. My brother might receive a call from a mechanic saying, "I like the prices you're giving me for filters and brake parts, but why are your prices higher for belts, hoses and shocks?" At that point, my brother would have to be able to point out that our line of shocks is of higher quality than our competitor's and that we can get that belt to him ten minutes faster than the competition, or we would have to meet the competitor's price.

Production depends on the continuous cooperation of vast numbers of people who are strangers to each other. We sourced our parts from more than 100 different suppliers over the course of a year. This doesn't count the vendors of other products and services. (utilities, gasoline, office supplies, etc.). Each supplier, in turn, had many sources for its inputs, and so on, going all the way back to the people who physically create and fabricate everything that goes into making the products. Tens of thousands of people cooperated to bring the part you need to you. The activities of these people need to be synchronized in terms of the timing of their readiness, the proportions of multiple inputs, and the availability of existing capital goods. All this has to be done while swiftly and continuously taking into account all of the various possible alternative uses for these inputs. Only the emergence of market prices makes this task possible. Market prices provide the information needed to plan and adjust production, while also providing the incentive to produce and to innovate. Monkeying with market prices is a bad idea. Inflation, especially, falsifies relative prices and falsifies the most important prices – interest rates. The resulting dysfunction, often wrongly blamed on the free market, spawns regulations and taxes that make matters worse.

The value of a capital good is completely dependent on the value it creates for customers. If you're not creating value for your customers, you cease to possess capital. In this light, we considered equipment purchases carefully. We monitored the size and composition of our inventory each day. Our largest cash outlay was always reinvestment in inventory, something that doesn't happen automatically, but is a conscious decision. There is always the possibility of capital being consumed or becoming worthless if you are not watchful. Lack of profit is a signal that the goods employed in the business should be released to someone better able to use them.

Business firms are mortal. A firm will die if customers no longer want its products. A firm will die if the employees aren't persuaded to show up each day ready to work. A firm will die if managers hijack the organization to make it serve their own purposes. A firm will die if entrepreneurs cease to be alert to challenges and opportunities. A firm will die if savers withdraw their capital. Successful business firms create a team to fulfill a mission in an environment where anyone may leave and no one has the power to coerce anyone to stay. It is this liberty, this voluntary cooperation, that creates successful organizations. All the players, from customers to bond holders, learn to adjust to each other's wants and assess each other's contributions. Sometimes the process is messy, but that's how it comes to work. If successful, everyone works together for the benefit of all.

In a pure free market, there is no ruling class. Each person's role in the economy, (subject to any constraints he puts on himself), is chosen by consumers, and these consumers want a wide and everchanging variety of things. No one has the power to preserve his position by force. This is the fundamental distinction between market societies and status societies of bureaucracy, caste, serfdom, slavery and all the current variants of market suppressing privilege.

Open your eyes and see that free economies are the best places. In surveys that rank countries according to the amount of economic freedom, the countries that come out on top are also the most prosperous countries and the places where most people want to live.

Free people make better people. The liberty to decide whether or not to make exchanges with others attenuates the scope of evil. When people are free to decide with whom to cooperate, psychopaths, sadists and bigots come to lack customers and employees, which is why evil people tend to lurk in bureaucracies. Examples are legion, but I was especially struck by this when reading Robert Caro's biography of Lyndon Johnson. Caro portrays Johnson as someone who chose politics over a business career because in politics he could gratify his deep-seated need to humiliate people.

On two occasions I can remember, people told me that, since I was in business, I made my living by cheating people. Goodness knows, there are people in business who are dishonest, but such people are to be found everywhere, even in those lines of work honored for their "selfless service." I am in agreement with the economist Benjamin Rogge's observation, "A basically dishonest man can survive longer in the church or the classroom than he can in the grain exchange or the furniture business."

Business II

"The auto parts business is simple," our father said, "You buy a part for a certain amount of money, and then you sell it for more." Saying that, he decamped after a couple months and turned operations over to my brother and me. We paid him for the inventory over the course of about twenty years, including interest, but he gave us the fixtures and a couple of old delivery trucks.

I grant that auto parts is more simple than farming or renting motel rooms.

We didn't have to worry about the weather or the price of our crop, and we weren't open 24/7 with our customers lodged all around us. But there is more to every trade than the layman realizes.

My brother, Buzz, who bore the brunt of the responsibility, was 22 at the time, had majored in politics, and was thinking of becoming a journalist. Neither of us was a "gear head" automobile enthusiast. I changed the oil in my car twice and have performed no further mechanical operations since. (Years later, when I was dating my wife, she noticed the cable of my emergency brake disassembled at her feet when she got into my car. "I thought you owned an auto parts store," was her dry comment. Let the record show that she was warned.)

My brother and I shouldered our new responsibilities. I secured the office. Buzz was a quick study on the operations side. From the counter sales people he learned the catalogues and the basic principles of internal combustion engines. Within a few weeks, we went from the customers saying, "Let me talk to anyone except Buzz," to, "Let me talk to Buzz."

For much of the time over the years, we would be training someone. I don't mean teaching new drivers the routes or teaching experienced people our line codes. I mean offering our delivery drivers the opportunity to learn the counter and increase their earning power. Whenever it was slow, the experienced people would give a lesson. Those trainees who were motivated were successful.

My bank experience prepared me to deal with the employer tax requirements. Besides federal and state income tax withholding, there are six other payroll taxes: Social Security, Medicare, state unemployment, federal unemployment, state disability insurance, and the employee training tax. (Workers' Compensation is an insurance mandate, rather than a tax. Because it benefits all parties, one would expect it to exist even if the mandate were withdrawn.)

The employee training tax creates a state fund that is disbursed to organizations doing training. Now, it doesn't pay a small business that intermittently trains one person at a time to apply for a grant, so our training efforts went uncompensated. But the Bank of America down the street received money from the fund for its teller school. In other words, the employee training tax transfers money from small businesses to big businesses to fund what the big business would have done anyway.

*

On an hour-to-hour basis, I had a lot of freedom to decide how to use my time. There was no supervisor standing over my shoulder, but there were always deadlines looming that had to be met. Payroll needed to be on time and accurate. Vendors that allowed an early payment discount had to be paid by the 10th of each month. The others had to be paid by the end of the month to avoid finance charges. The bills to our customers had to go out on time. Checking credit, opening accounts, setting account limits, collecting bad debts, and sometimes going to small claims court were part of my job. There was no assistant to help me, so taking a couple days of off required planning ahead. In any case, checking how the business was doing and keeping up with routine tasks, as well as making the occasional delivery to keep our service first rate, had me going in for at least an hour or two almost every Saturday and Sunday. Living a five-minute drive or a fifteen minute walk from work made this easy. I would almost always go home for lunch.

The most unforgiving deadlines, after payroll, were tax deadlines, and there were a lot of them. My personal tax deadlines included property tax payments and my state and federal personal returns, along with quarterly estimated payments. The business required monthly sales tax returns, quarterly sales tax returns and maintaining a file of customers who were resellers, regular state and federal payroll tax deposits, quarterly state and federal payroll tax returns, maintaining a file of W-4s, the annual payroll reconciliation return and W-2s, an annual business license "fee" that was, in fact, a gross receipts tax, and our state and federal partnership returns. For large swaths of my time at work, I felt as if I'd been absorbed into the state bureaucracy, rather like the Borg in *Star Trek*.

All this paperwork places a disproportionately large burden on small businesses; the paperwork cost of six employees is more than 10% of the paperwork cost of sixty employees. I remember my mother complaining about our one employee at our motel triggering all the payroll tax return requirements. Someone with a one-man repair shop might be reluctant to hire a helper because of the burden. Even if you outsource your bookkeeping, it's still an expense.

The inflation of the late 1970s produced a string of state tax revolt movements. It is no accident that these were directed against property taxes. Property taxes are paid directly and in a lump sum. They are not hidden. Most of our tax system, by contrast, is designed to make the taxes we pay as hidden as possible. Federal Income Tax Withholding by the employer began as a war measure during World War Two, but it was continued after the war ended. If income taxes were due in one lump sum, rather than withheld, people would likely rebel against the tax, but when taxes are taken out of each paycheck, the taxpayer comes to think of the net pay as his or her pay and forgets about the tax, as Vivien Kellems pointed out years ago.

The social security tax is also deducted from paychecks rather than being paid directly by the taxpayer. Not only that, but the taxpayer doesn't see half of the burden since half of the tax is hidden as the "employer's share" and doesn't appear on the paystub. The distribution of the benefits is also misleading. Social Security benefits are paid out as soon as they are collected, but you are simultaneously promised money in the future. So, a 50 cent deduction you see on your paycheck is only half of the one dollar of total tax. That dollar is given to Grandma and another dollar is promised to you. As a result, it looks to the wage-earner like the government has found a way to turn 50 cents into two dollars.

The sales tax is another largely hidden tax. We are aware of it when we buy a big-ticket item, but most of the time we don't think about it. Well, I thought about it a lot because of the thousands of dollars of collected sales tax I had to send in each month. The sales tax is not easy to collect. There are a lot of rules and rulings around what is taxable and what is not, each of them a potential source of campaign contributions from favored or threatened industries. The rules on freight are confusing. On the one hand, freight is not taxable. On the other hand, there are rules to guard against putting non-freight charges into the freight category. We had to maintain a file of resale cards from customers claiming (Honestly? Who knows?) to be resellers and therefore exempt. And we would sell in jurisdictions with different rates, something difficult to track.

The most disturbing thing about the sales tax is the hypocrisy of it. The "trump card" that is pulled from the deck to justify any tax is that the tax is necessary to improve the lot of the poor. Yet the sales tax is a regressive tax; *it disproportionately harms the poor*. Moreover, it is a broad-based tax that makes it difficult for people suffering from poor schools and poor policing to arrange to buy these services directly.

*

David Graeber has written that there are many jobs in our economy that may politely be described as "BS jobs." While we might debate which jobs are included in this category, the tax industry certainly qualifies. Look at the Federal Income tax. When this tax takes a dollar, that dollar doesn't magically disappear from the taxpayer's bank account to appear later at a congressional committee meeting. Things are *done* to people – costly things. There are compliance costs (learning about the tax laws, record keeping, preparing returns, processing returns), there are enforcement costs (audits, litigation, forced collections, imprisonment), there are evasion and avoidance costs (tax shelters, lobbying, the inefficiencies of black markets), and disincentive costs (work not performed and investments not made because taxes reduced the return.) As an example of a compliance cost, my barber's accountant wanted $400. to prepare her returns.

In 1993, political scientist and researcher James Payne wrote a book, *Costly Returns: The Burdens of the U.S. Tax System*, in which he gathered data from several studies and made some reasonable calculations of his own to estimate that the federal income tax costs $1.65 for every dollar the government collects. The dollar in net revenue comes with 65 cents in costs, with compliance costs and disincentive costs making up most of the total. There is no reason to believe this figure has improved since. Even if one claims that Payne has overestimated by a factor of two, and adds the dubious assumption that all the tasks government undertakes are necessary and performed efficiently, it is clear that the federal income tax industry destroys a tremendous amount of potential production. The only economic "good" taxes produce in abundance is power for those people who relish power.

A friend of mine was selected for audit by the I.R.S. They found that his return was all correct, so he was a little surprised when his return was selected for audit again the following year. Once again, he passed the audit with no problems. When his return was selected for audit the third year in a row, his accountant wrote a letter to the I.R.S. claiming harassment. This time they backed off. My friend doesn't know why he was singled out three times. Maybe the agent had it in for him.

The California Franchise Tax Board didn't post one of my payments. I called them to ask for help and was given incorrect advice on how to fix the problem. A few months later, I tried again. Once again, I was given incorrect advice. By now they had seized money out of my bank account. The third person I called finally told me how to fix the problem. She also cautioned me never to send the tax board correspondence. They were dealing with their mail three months after receiving it.

Educated people, financially savvy people, people who can afford to hire professionals to help them – have some ability to navigate the bureaucracy. I have seen a couple of people who don't have these advantages get caught in tax hell. It isn't pretty.

Why I am Not a Social Democrat

Most ideological debates amount to nothing more than signaling virtue or tribal membership. Words like "capitalism," "globalism," and "neoliberalism" are subject to so many different, even contradictory, definitions that those who use them in debate end up with no understanding of each other's positions. Shadings such as "American Capitalism," "Late Capitalism," and "Finance Capitalism" add to the confusion. Even such a neutral-sounding word as "individualism" is slippery. Does one mean ontological individualism, ethical individualism, or methodological individualism? One author I read used "individualism" as a synonym for "selfishness;" one could replace "individualism" with "selfishness" in every line and capture his meaning exactly. Compare this with another author who is using the term "individualism" to discuss freedom of choice, or legal responsibility, or each soul's accountability.

I therefore risk misunderstanding by titling this "Why I am Not a Social Democrat." Do I mean the Social Democrats of Germany in 1900, or of Sweden in 1970, or something else? The best way to dispel confusion is to list what I take to be the key institutions of American Social Democracy, even if this list is not commonly given that name.

First, that complex of laws designed to increase the earnings of labor: compulsory unionism, minimum wages, mandated benefits.

Secondly, a universal, compulsory tax tied to a promise of benefits in old age.

Third, taxes combined with restrictions on free contracts tied to the promise of better health care.

Fourth, taxation tied to the promise that education will be produced with the proceeds.

None of these promises are binding legal contracts.

What could possibly go wrong?

Let's begin with labor. The level of wages is determined by the productivity of labor. Each employer will continue hiring labor as long as the extra revenue the last worker produces is more than the wage rate. Each employer competes for labor with the other employers, who are doing the same. Labor is constantly being shifted to what consumers consider to be its most productive use, and each worker is drawn to the place where he or she earns the highest wage (or best total compensation package, including the location, the schedule, how interesting the work is, etc.) Increased productivity makes goods more abundant, prices fall, and real wages (purchasing power) rise.

Workers are made more productive by the availability of savings embodied in capital goods (all the various kinds of tools and skills that can be brought to bear) and by the productive plans implemented by alert and innovative entrepreneurs. Savers, who forgo consumption to make resources available, and entrepreneurs are the heroes of the economy. Workers who take the time to acquire skills they think will be valuable are also acting as savers and entrepreneurs.

Taxing savers and entrepreneurs strikes at the heart of economic progress. Their efforts make goods more abundant and cheaper. (Cheaper if we had sound money!) The amount of money savers earn is limited by the rate of time preference; the more willing people are to wait for the fruits of their labor, the more interest rates fall and the lower the return savers receive. Successful entrepreneurs who create new industries or reinvent old ones can earn large profits, but these tend, absent government protection, to be competed away over time, and unsuccessful entrepreneurs are punished with losses. Hence there are natural limits to what the patient saver and the restless entrepreneur can earn. The bulk of the increased production they make possible flows to the workers, even to the most prodigal and unambitious.

Increased production can't be conjured out of the air by passing a law. Attempts to force a redistribution to the workers by means of price control fail. This is best illustrated with an example: Suppose a minimum wage is established for homecare givers that is above the market rate – the rate at which all willing buyers and sellers make a bargain. At the above-market rate, some of the buyers drop out of the market; they can't afford to buy as much as before. Family members must be called upon to provide the service, or people do without. The people these frustrated buyers would have hired are now unemployed. These unemployed either drop out of the labor market or they offer their services in other industries (or in the black market for labor), where they drive wages down for the workers there. Supporters of minimum wages focus on the people who remain employed at a higher wage. But for a true picture of the situation, you need to consider the losses of the people who are prevented from buying what they want and the workers priced out of the market who become unemployed or shift wages lower elsewhere.

A general minimum wage reduces production through job losses or reduced hours worked, and that reduced production cannot help but make workers as a whole worse off. Powerful labor unions have the same effect. Labor unions, of course, perform more than one function, and people have the right to form voluntary associations. But in most cases people part with their union dues and vote in union elections with a view to securing a wage rate above the market rate. Deleterious consequences for workers as a whole follow. Employment is reduced. If the union succeeds in reducing the return on capital in a firm or industry, that firm or industry attracts less capital in the future. With less capital, workers are less productive than they otherwise would have been, and that firm or industry declines relative to the others. Even as payrolls shrink, the current generation of workers, with their short time horizon, may not care. This is why private sector unions have been declining; their jobs tend to disappear. Only the public sector unions, with their power to coerce transfers, continue to grow.

The politics of unions is also important. Unions are subject to all the pathologies of democratic decision making. The incumbent union officials control the treasury and the union newsletter, and they can devote paid time to maintaining their control. The "Iron Law of Oligarchy," – the insight that majorities never rule organizations because a small cabal always sets the agenda – asserts itself, and the organization is often run for the benefit of a few. To establish and maintain themselves, unions need favorable rulings from the National Labor Relations Board on the definition of bargaining units, on jurisdictional disputes, and on unfair labor practices. This puts them at the mercy of the politicians who appoint the members of the National Labor Relations Board. There is therefore a tendency for union officials to become cogs in the political machine.

Because the total wage package that workers receive is determined by productivity, "mandated benefits," such as requiring paid family leave, are paid for by reduced wages. Mandated benefits simply reduce the workers' range of choices. In the case of paid family leave, the lower wage rate may actually cause a parent to be at work, rather than at home, for more hours than he or she otherwise would because the lifetime wages of the parents are reduced by the mandate. This is seen even more clearly when family leave is paid for by higher taxes—people may respond to the tax by spending more time working and less time with family.

Advocates of "laborism" sometimes argue that employers can exploit labor through their superior bargaining power. But, as we have seen, it pays employers to make more and higher wage offers as long as marginal productivity justifies it. To refrain from making higher offers just to keep the wage rate low does not pay, and even if one employer foolishly did so, the other employers would eagerly step up and fill the gap.

Ultimately, it is the consumers who hire the workers. Employers have to give their employees the sad news, "Sorry, but our customers won't pay enough for me to pay you more." And employers have to give their customers the sad news, "Sorry, but our employees won't work cheaply enough for me to lower prices." Being the voice of reality doesn't make one popular.

*

The next three major institutions of American social democracy – social security, Medicare, and public schools – are usually defended on the grounds that some people need financial help. Yet their salient feature is that they are universal in scope. Why not simply have welfare for the aged poor, as existed before social security? Why not a means-tested Medicare? Why not scholarships for poor students? *Why must everyone be forced to pay for everyone?* Why must every dollar spent on these things make a round-trip through politics?

A number of concerns motivated the originators of these programs. Some feared that taxpayers would be too stingy if money were earmarked for the poor alone, and hoped that extra benefits for the poor could be embedded in a universal program. Others wanted to prepare the people for a socialist future – to get every family accustomed to receiving a portion of its income in the form of a government check. This would break the link between market transactions/voluntary transfers and income. Eventually the coercive sector would grow until it encompassed the entire economy, the ultimate goal of the socialists. They also wanted to destroy proud self-reliance. The stigma of receiving charity would be replaced by the vigorous assertion of rights to things.

Socialists, even when they whisper into the ear of power, cannot put these programs over with their arguments alone. *Social democracy is established because it serves the needs of political elites.* There are patronage jobs here, of course, but the main function of these programs is to make people dependent on the existence of a powerful state – to reconcile them to heavy taxation, debt, and the machinations of the central bank, and to make them willing soldiers. Once these institutions are firmly established, political elites are able to exercise unaccountable power. With state education thrown into the mix, it becomes almost impossible for dissenting voices to gain ground.

The flaws inherent in coercive (no exit allowed!) institutions soon became manifest. Social Security quickly became a Ponzi scheme. Funds that should have been set aside for the future were spent today, making the system a bad deal for future workers. Health care is almost totally detached from the price system; you might as well spin a Wheel-of-Fortune to find out what things cost. In the schools your children are taught what the authorities want them to be taught, and there is little accountability if reading and writing aren't on the list.

Yet each new generation finds it difficult to imagine alternatives to the system into which they have been born. What might an alternative to Social Security look like? Imagine entering the workforce and buying a whole-life-and-disability insurance policy. The premium you pay each month is invested in productive capital goods, generating rising wages and lower prices. If you live to retire and see your children grown, you no longer need the insurance protection and can convert the policy into a life annuity. It's fully funded with assets and lasts for life. Why do so few people do this? Because government promises have lulled them into complacency, because they can't afford the premiums after paying the social security tax, and because Federal Reserve created inflation has severely crippled the annuity market.

Under Social Democracy, your employment contracts are written by someone else, your savings are handed over to politicos, your doctor ultimately doesn't work for you, and your child's teacher doesn't work for you. Humans are reduced to sheep in a world made for their shepherds – shepherds whose ambition to control us eventually knows no bounds.

Liberty means having our *human* lives returned to us.

Education

The Baymont Christian School Homeschool Program was destroyed. Let me explain.

There are three ways to homeschool legally in California. The first is to register your home with the state as a school. This is simple. You fill out a brief form and send it in. You tell them who you are and promise to have a lesson plan and keep attendance records, but you don't actually need to send in a copy of your plan or your records.

The second way is to affiliate your homeschool with an existing private school. Generally, the private school will want to know that you are a responsible person, will check in with you periodically, and will administer achievement tests.

The third way to homeschool is to go through the local public school and follow an approved curriculum.

When my wife and I decided to homeschool our daughter, we began by sending her to a private part-time kindergarten/ first grade designed to supplement homeschooling. From grades two through eight, she was homeschooled full-time. She also took art classes at a small art school, played in a soccer league, took piano lessons, and was involved in church activities.

We did not want to register our home as a private school, in spite of the minimal requirements. It would mean putting ourselves on a database in Sacramento at a time when homeschoolers felt vulnerable to a crackdown on what they were doing. There was reason to be wary. The right to homeschool was fairly new. It had been fought for, and not just in the courtroom. There had been a homeschool "civil rights movement" in the 1970s and 80s. In some places, children were temporarily taken from their parents and parents put in jail until the local outcry, usually led by churches, caused the authorities to back off. Teachers' unions wanted to restrict homeschooling to parents with teaching credentials. Sometimes an educator would opine that homeschooling was *prima facia* evidence of child abuse and probable cause for an investigation by Child Protective Services. But as the sheer number of families homeschooling grew, it became politically impossible to put a stop to it.

We did not want to homeschool through the public school because we wanted the freedom to choose our own curriculum. So, we were led to the private school affiliation option. Our first sponsor was Baymont Christian School. The person in charge of the program there was very helpful, and the program as a whole had an excellent reputation. There were more than two hundred families signed up.

Then the local public school began offering $1,000. of financial aid to any family that would drop Baymont and affiliate with the government school. One condition for signing up was to produce sufficient work free of religious content. We didn't want to submit to regulation of our curriculum or burden the taxpayers, so we said "no." Only about twenty families joined us in saying "no," too few for Baymont to continue to employ a homeschool liaison, so Baymont's homeschool program folded, the victim of a competitor with tax money to spend.

After much searching, we found a church in Hollister that sponsored homeschools, so we signed up with them. This program grew to the point where the church felt it no longer had the time to do an adequate job of monitoring all its affiliates, and rather than engage in the thankless task of deciding who was in and who was not, it shut down its entire program.

With only a couple years left before choosing a high school, it looked like we would have to register our home with the state, but my wife had become acquainted with one of the Hollister mothers who had registered her home as a school. Knowing that we were doing a good job, she was glad to call our home one of her school's satellite locations. We did not pay her anything for this favor, and our only contact was to meet with her once a year by phone.

*

The major educational benefit of homeschooling is that each lesson is tailor made to where the student is at each moment. If something is too hard, you can immediately downshift to a more elementary level, and if something is too easy, you can go right to more advanced work. You can stay on the cusp of the student's interest. If a particular topic fires the student's imagination, you can do nothing but that topic for a week. If a subject is boring, you can leave it aside until the student clearly sees the need to learn it.

Freeing the child from the classroom opens up possibilities for travel, field trips, supplemental special classes, interaction with people of all ages, positive socialization (instead of peer pressure), and learning life skills.

Homeschooling is not for everyone or all the time. Some choose it for the earliest grades alone. Others choose it for middle school alone. Many would like to homeschool but, between taxes and the crippled markets that make housing and medical care expensive, they need to work full time just to provide for their children's basic needs.

There is a missing option in schooling. It isn't difficult for me to set up a home school for my own children, but if a neighbor hires me to add her or his child to my class, there are obstacles. Zoning regulations and regulations against home businesses may prevent it. The license and tax requirements are a hurdle.

There may be regulations in the name of safety that are onerous. (Surely the very young must be looked out for, but once a child is street wise and articulate, going next door to learn is no less safe that going next door to play.) The missing option in schooling is the small neighborhood private school held in someone's home.

*

The government spends an average of around $14,000 per year for each child in the public schools, with a range from $8,000 to $24,000, depending on the state. When schooling is purchased through taxes, people seldom think about the cost. Lifting this tax burden and opening up competition between private schools would turn millions of parents into price-shoppers. And there is every reason to expect the quality of education to rise as well, with a plethora of new options arising and every incentive for them to provide quality instruction. *When it comes to achieving results, incentives matter more than total dollars spent.*

*

Our choice of schooling should be guided by more than a simple cost/quality calculation. We need to be able to choose what our children are taught. And if this results in teaching a wide diversity of viewpoints, occasionally even distasteful ones, remember that free societies tend to foster both tolerance and learning from each other when those young people go out into the world and need to trade and interact voluntarily with people who think differently. The government schools teach inescapable group conflict and then they release those children into a bureaucratic/ zero sum landscape that fosters conflict.

The fatal flaw in all charter school and tax-funded voucher schemes is that they pay for schooling with tax dollars. *Tax dollars mean loss of control.* They also inevitably mean that state supremacy is taught. Minds are nationalized. State Education becomes the new State Church. With hindsight, we can see that once the state fastened its grip on the banks and the schools in the 19th century, the long decline of liberty became inevitable.

These edifices are now too strong to yield to frontal assault, no matter what voting rules we adopt. But they might be circumvented. Just as having decentralized, sound money payments systems would put us beyond control by the banking system, so having thousands of small independent schools forming and dissolving as needed would put us, and the best teachers, beyond control by the education bureaucracy.

John Kimball

Admired though I may be, I am not the heroic figure in my wife's life. That role belongs to her father, John Kimball. Around the time I met him, she described him to me as a mixture of Cary Grant, John Wayne, and Dr. Albert Schweitzer. As I got to know him, I could see why.

John Kimball was born in North Dakota but grew up in Los Angeles. Circumstances made him the main breadwinner of his family as a teenager. He worked his way through college (you could do that back then) working in the oil fields and as a film extra, among other jobs. He served at the San Diego Naval Hospital in World War II as a medical corpsman, and graduated with an MD from Stanford after the war. He was drafted again during the Korean War (leaving a wife and young son at home) and served at a hospital in Japan.

He settled in Tracy, California, in 1954, at that time a town of about 10,000 people. This is where my wife and a second daughter were born. He had the practice of a small-town physician of his day. He was a Family Practitioner, seeing about 50 patients per day. He also did OB/Gyn, and delivered more than 3,000 babies during the course of his career. He was a General Surgeon, performing many surgeries, and thanks to his experience in military hospitals, he did orthopedics. He was "on call" as emergency room physician more than one night a week, often getting up in the middle of the night to go to the hospital three blocks away. And he did house calls. He was also the team physician for the high school football team for 40 years, an unpaid volunteer job.

Dr. Kimball practiced medicine for about ten years before

Medicare began. The doctors in Tracy were a close-knit group. They would work together in their practices. They would see each other at church or the Rotary Club. Their children went to school together. Their families often got together.

Since the medical care a person receives can't be resold to someone else, doctors have the ability to charge on a sliding-scale and give their low-income patients a price break. Each doctor in Tracy was expected by the others to help a certain number of patients with low fee or even free care. If one of the doctors in town was not pulling his share of the load, another doctor would pull him aside and say, "We don't think you're picking up your share of the charity patients." With his reputation at stake, the doctor who heard this would quickly shoulder more of the load.

The advent of medical insurance made it more difficult for doctors to help the poor though price discrimination. Insurance reimbursements are based on what a doctor charges his patients. If he gives discounts to his low-income patients, that reduces the base from which his insurance payments for his other patients are calculated. Direct help to the poor in the form of his care becomes more costly.

*

Governments have every incentive to regulate in favor of organized producers rather than unorganized consumers, limiting supply to raise prices. Health care is no exception. American Medical Association control over the accreditation of medical schools has been used to limit the supply of doctors. A longer period of time is required to train a physician in the United States than in other developed countries. In some states, a "certificate of need" from regulators is required to expand hospital services.

The battle for control of the market was also fought against doctors who worked for a group of patients for a salary and against doctors who advertised their prices. On the demand side, doctors and hospitals lobbied against insurance plans that indemnified patients a fixed sum of money for routine diagnoses and procedures and favored "open checkbook" plans instead.

Doctors want to keep their licenses to practice. They want to keep their specialty certification. They want membership in the county medical society and hospital privileges. These are "choke points" the bureaucracy can squeeze if a doctor doesn't follow the current party line.

A vast increase in the amount of medical care paid by insurance began during World War II. War industries wanted to hire more workers, but price controls on wages prevented employers from making offers that would draw workers to where they were needed. Benefits, however, up to a limit, were exempt from price controls, so employer-paid health insurance became a popular means of compensation. In addition, the IRS ruled that, while employers could deduct the cost of the benefit, employees did not have to pay income or payroll taxes on it. With high tax rates persisting after the war ended, employer-paid health insurance grew. Because of this tax boon, traditional insurance – real insurance, insurance that pays for random, catastrophic events – was replaced by insurance for all things medical. Much of the incentive to economize in buying care was removed, and the increase in demand pushed up prices. The paperwork burden also increased. Moreover, state legislators began to add "mandated benefits" to insurance contracts. These require certain benefits to be in the contract or that contract is illegal. Interest groups from wig makers to chiropractors piled on, driving up the cost of insurance and making it less affordable. All of this pushed up the price of health care for those who did not have employer coverage, i.e., the retired and the aged. The stage was set for Medicare.

*

My family didn't have health insurance until 1970. Before then, we simply saved our money in order to be prepared to pay medical bills. We finally bought medical insurance to cover anything big that might come along. Unfortunately, people today seldom think in terms of protection from large expenses; they think in terms of getting "free stuff" from their employer's plan. Employees are more likely to compare notes on the out-of-pocket cost of an exam than on their coverage for a long hospital stay.

*

There seems a certain inevitability in our march toward a system where the government pays all medical bills. I've had intelligent people tell me flatly that there is "no alternative." Many young people have embraced what I call "meet the mail carrier" socialism. Under this system, whenever the mail carrier tries to hand you a bill for medical care or school tuition, you simply write "Please forward to Washington D.C" on it and hand it back. Problem solved.

Free market alternatives are outside the bounds of most public discussion. You need to search to find them presented. A number of reforms are implied in what I have written above. Probably the most effective first step would be to abolish all taxes on work, both income and payroll (No, not by creating a new consumption tax!) Abolishing all taxes on work would, besides increasing the return on a medical education and hence the supply of professionals, make it attractive for employees to take more compensation in cash and less in health insurance. The resulting decline in third-party payment for health care would open up the field for entrepreneurs to provide healthcare directly to the patients, and there is evidence that this would, in many cases, greatly reduce prices.

Concierge medicine, with its direct payment from patients to doctors, and prepaid contracts to provide care, provided these are not regulated as "insurance," have proven they can deliver cost savings. Surgery centers owned by doctors, such as the renowned Surgery Center of Oklahoma, can deliver large cost savings for non-emergency surgery and would save us from that trip to a hospital in Singapore or Panama that some make for such surgery today and many more would make under single-payer. There are people working on providing generic drugs without a "benefits manager." This promises savings as well. These innovations are easy to envision. More radical reformers want to reexamine occupational licensure and drug patents, but I don't know enough about these to comment on them.

*

I know a man who always wanted to be a doctor, but he was not admitted to medical school. There is a good chance he would have been admitted had he been Hispanic because it was a year when the medical schools were scrambling to admit a more diverse student body. What did he do? He applied to the Medical School at the University of Guadalajara *in Mexico* and was admitted. Some of the faculty there resented the presence of American students at their school, thinking they were taking places that should have gone to Mexicans. Perhaps so. Or maybe the tuition dollars they brought in created more places for Mexican students. In any case, after he graduated, he joined a practice where, as the only doctor who spoke Spanish, he saw all the Hispanic patients. His foreign education improved care for the Mexican Americans of his state. In fact, he was so fluent in Spanish, and with his dark hair and moustache, some of his patients thought they were seeing a Mexican doctor. (A doctor who "looks like us?")

There are a large number of human characteristics upon which one could base an affirmative action program in higher education, and the results, both good and bad, might vary in interesting and unpredictable ways, as my story above illustrates. The worst policy is for the government to force every school to do the same thing, especially when that becomes a narrow debate about race and merit. *The solution is the separation of school and state and freedom for each school to do as it wishes.* Consumers should then demand transparency from each school on its policies and their results.

*

During the 1950s, Dr. Kimball became acquainted with a young black man who was headed for medical school but didn't have money to pay for it. Kimball paid his tuition, and the young man became a doctor.

*

Doctor Kimball retired from his private practice at the age of 71. He continued to serve as a volunteer medical director at Hospice and as a member of the Hospital Foundation Board until he was 83. They named a high school and a park after him. These honors are usually reserved for people who write big donation checks, but he was not honored in exchange for a check. He was honored for being the kind of man he was.

Those Social Issues

In his book, *Excellent Sheep*, William Deresiewicz laments that he doesn't know how to talk with his plumber. There is too much of a social gap, he feels, between himself, a Professor of English who taught at Yale, and the person who comes to his house to fix something for them to have anything to say to each other.

In our democratic age, we find our fears in what we imagine to be the "average person." Conservatives see people as prone to envy. Modern liberals see people as primed to hate anyone who is different. I haven't spent a lot of time chatting with someone dealing with the plumbing, but during over thirty years of working in our old-fashioned auto parts store with its comfortable stools lined up along the counter, I heard a lot of "bull sessions" among mechanics, tradesmen, and people who work on their own cars. I am happy to report that the average person is not seething with envy or with hatred of the "Other." Most just want to get through their day. Sometimes my brother would be the only college graduate I would speak with all day. Those were usually the days when I heard the most good sense spoken.

Politics makes us afraid of each other. Votes are potential weapons. Even if we hold a small cabal to be responsible for our poor governance, we fear majorities because they are responsible for allowing it, even endorsing it, at the ballot box.

We should resist drawing from this the lesson that people can't be trusted with their *own* lives. What we can't trust people with is *other* people's lives. Ignorance and credulity are the rule here. Bryan Caplan got it right: Our political disfunction is best explained by assuming that people who cast votes are radically ignorant and people who seek votes are radically evil.

*

My in-laws' house in Aptos has a large yard that needs to be weeded every spring. Most years the family and I do it, but twice I have hired a day laborer to help me with the job. One year the man the labor exchange sent was an especially hard worker, and he smiled proudly when I complained I couldn't keep up with him. On the other occasion I offered the man they sent some food at our lunch break. He smiled, pulled out his thermos and said warmly, "No thanks. My wife makes me a good soup." These men were telling me, 'I do valuable work," and "My family loves and cares for me." This is where they found happiness, the happiness of satisfaction, the happiness that is a fruit of virtue – "status rewards" and "social capital" in the bloodless jargon of sociologists, but the pith of our lives.

*

There were other conversations with employees that did not merit pride. This scenario played out *twice* (two different young men):

A young man working for us enters my office, closes the door and sits down.

"I need an advance of $XXX. On my paycheck."

"What for?"

"Well, my girlfriend, she has a problem."

"A problem?"

"She needs an abortion."

I suppress a grimace and assume a formal, businesslike demeanor, both to avoid an awkward scene and to distance myself from what I'm doing.

"Give me your time card."

We sit there silently as I add up his hours and multiply them by his rate of pay, including the overtime.

"You have enough coming to cover what you want."

I write him a check and he quickly leaves.

*

I don't know when I first heard about same-sex marriage. It was probably after I turned thirty. My sense is that before that time, many gay people would have dismissed the idea saying, "We have our own ways. We're not interested in imitating the customs of the 'breeders.'" There was a latent case for same-sex marriage that grew stronger over the years as the state grew. Same-sex marriage would have been useful when next-of-kin was an issue and when people died intestate. The estate tax sometimes made it valuable to be a spouse. The income tax made joint returns attractive. Employer provided health insurance (an artifact of the tax laws) made family coverage a desirable benefit. Social Security spousal benefits reward the married. The issue might have remained dormant had it not been for the AIDS epidemic. The horrific impact of this event reminded Gays of the ways in which the law did not treat them the same way it treated other people.

I supported same-sex marriage when that was a minority viewpoint. If two people, competent and not minors, want to write a marriage contract and deposit a copy with a third party designated by them to adjudicate any disputes, why should they not be free to do so? As long as no one is prohibited from celebrating or compelled to celebrate their union, it is their own business.

Conservatives object to being characterized as mindless supporters of the status quo, saying, "We don't want to preserve *everything*. We only want to preserve the *permanent things*," which raises the question, "What are the permanent things?" One answer is to reason from natural law, but once natural law theory goes beyond certain basics (self-ownership, for example) it becomes difficult to work it out. Another approach is evolutionary.

The institutions free people adopt over time are likely to serve genuine human needs.

Same-sex marriage swept to a surprisingly swift victory. Appeals to fairness and sentiment won most people over. Political elites were glad to integrate Gays into the tax and welfare state. (Better to pay more spousal benefits than to alienate a group of people from social security.) But the test of any institution is time. If we were to abolish the tax and welfare state and then see what happens over the next two or three generations, that would be a true test of same-sex marriage, and of many other things as well. Maybe same sex marriage would join the ranks of the permanent things. Or perhaps it would fade away. Maybe it would be common among lesbian couples with children, but otherwise rare. We won't have the answer in my lifetime.

*

Abortion and transgender issues generate the heated discussion. Meanwhile, quietly, seemingly inexorably, divorce, cohabitation, and single parenthood steadily weaken the family. (According to the research group Child Trends, as cited in the Wall Street Journal, about 40% of births in the United States occur outside marriage.) From the perch of my business office, it sometimes seemed to me that, for the bottom quarter or third of the income scale, the family is almost gone.

*

At some mainline Protestant churches, the sermons generally follow one of two themes: 1) We are too materialistic; and 2) We are not sufficiently friendly toward people who are different from us. You rarely hear a sermon on "Why you should get married and stay married," rather than reach for cohabitation or easy divorce. No wonder that, in California, so many people are now getting married in wineries rather than churches.

*

I've had Marxists tell me that the family was doomed once *fathers* began working outside the home. Some traditionalist family-church-community conservatives date the doom of the family to those 18th century liberals who told the common man that liberty and the pursuit of happiness were within his grasp. The common man, on hearing this, supposedly began to neglect his duties.

Institutions thrive when they perform important functions. Family, churches, neighborhoods, and all the institutions of civil society, as many have said, *need to have work to do.* Marshall Fritz used to say that the two greatest anti-family institutions in America are Social Security and Public Education. They remove the family from intergenerational planning and reduce the potential benefits and responsibilities of parenthood.

Ever lengthening requirements for formal education delay adulthood. Life skills are not taught. Regulation of housing and inflationary finance reduce the affordability of housing and make it difficult to form a household. Regulation of medical care raises prices and makes it difficult to provide for a family. Taxes confiscate the fruits of labor, making it difficult to be self-supporting. Inflation makes it difficult to save, as cash melts away. Men can't fulfill their family roles and some despair. Some women "marry the state," which is simply a shorthand way of saying that the state comes to replace the family.

A man of about thirty who worked for us for a while as a retail clerk and later worked as a service writer at a repair shop once said to me, "I'll probably never marry. What do I have to offer a woman?" Twice a month I was required to take money out of his paycheck and send it to the state.

*

Why marriage? Why not just cohabitation? I haven't studied sociology, but I know what my mother taught me: that marriage helps males to grow up and become men, rather than remain perpetual adolescents. It is how men and women come together to support each other in a long-term project – the most important long-term project, if they have children – and form another of those little platoons that make human society work. Ideally, they forge durable bonds of affection that serve as a haven when they find themselves in a heartless world.

In a free society, the family project is furthered. There is more scope to learn what works (or doesn't) from example. Non-governmental assistance in the form of family support, mutual aid, charity, and commercial insurance is usually coupled with admonitions and incentives to improve one's behavior. Sound money and the opportunity to acquire property through patient effort lengthens time horizons and discourages a "live for today" attitude. And, as a culture turns toward the virtues, those who practice them are increasingly paid with respect, both self-respect and the respect of others, respect often expressed most effectively in communities like churches. A good reputation, in turn, invites emulation and internalizes values.

*

I remember reading years ago about the revival of the Lutheran Church of Estonia after the breakup of the Soviet Union. The few old pastors who were still around and others of the older generation did not take the lead. The revival was spearheaded by women in their twenties. They were thinking about what the next generation, their children, needed, and trying to build it in a time of uncertainty.

*

Will the "atomization" of society continue, or will there be a reversal? I doubt that family, church, and community are coming back until there is massive disillusionment with the state.

Confronting the State

"Martin Luther King Jr. was the most successful politician in Twentieth Century America, and he never ran for office."

Nicholas von Hoffman was speaking to a roomful of us at a Libertarian Party of California convention around 1976. The crowd was young and intense and kept him for a question-and-answer session about twice as long as his presentation. The whole while von Hoffman chain-smoked and coughed violently, giving him the aura of someone telling the truth before dying.

Von Hoffman was a nationally syndicated columnist. As a young man he had worked for Saul Alinsky in Chicago, organizing all manner of protests and the occasional election campaign for the politically powerless. Always alert to discontent bubbling up and to the potential for radical change, von Hoffman was attracted to libertarianism as a serious and even revolutionary philosophy, yet one in the mainstream of the American tradition with potentially broad appeal.

To test the commitment of the crowd he asked, "How many of you engaged in draft resistance?" Almost half of the hands went up. He seemed surprised. "You have been infiltrated!" he said.

With a nod to the fact that he was at a political convention, von Hoffman began with a warning, "Most of the people you elect will betray you, thanks to that Old Demon, power." Then, referencing the fact that libertarianism is an intellectual movement as much as a political one, he gave us a dose of reality, "You don't accomplish anything by reading Ludwig von Mises to people standing in an unemployment line."

While some people may enjoy candidate politics and others enjoy intellectual debate, he told us, we need to focus on battles that pit liberty against power. This doesn't mean running to the head of the victory parade on those rare occasions where liberty is on the brink of winning. It means standing up for causes when they are unpopular and keeping faith in long-term success. "Go out and get your ticket punched," von Hoffman said. He told us that our principles and our understanding must be embodied in concrete actions on specific issues. Draw the connection to liberty in general, but only while you work for liberty case by case.

*

I was active in our local Libertarian Party for about twenty years. People who join the party tend to go through three stages. First, they think we are on the brink of rapid growth and victory. This attitude probably peaked in 1978 – 1980. When victory doesn't arrive, the fallback position is to say, "The party just needs to achieve the level of success that the Socialist Party had from 1910 – 1920: elect two or three congressmen, a couple dozen state legislators and a few hundred local officials and then the major parties will start adopting our positions." But the party has never elected a congress-member as a libertarian, the number of libertarians in state legislative seats at any one time fluctuates between one and six, and the hundred or so local officials it has serving at any one time invariably represent only the smallest jurisdictions. There is also the question of whether the Socialist Party analogy holds. After all, the socialists were urging politicians to do what they want to do anyway – seize more power; *of course,* their positions were adopted by the other parties.

Faced with the failure of any strategy that depends on electing candidates, the libertarian falls back to the position that the mission of the party is to "spread the ideas." This was actually a good plan when it was first advanced. Before the Internet, the only way to spread the ideas widely was in the context of an electoral campaign. Run a candidate and that candidate will be interviewed by newspapers, radio and television – free publicity just at the time when the public is paying attention. And campaigns can be used to build your mailing list. The danger is that a crazy person might file to run, successfully grab your party's line on the ballot, and then use your microphone to spread his own theories – that "libertarians believe the earth is flat" or something.

The advent of the Internet made it possible to spread ideas at low cost without having to run candidates for office. Moreover, you could retain 100 percent control over the message you put out on your website. So why do you need a party at all? A party organization can provide two benefits. It can be a social club that facilitates local libertarians getting together and talking with each other face to face, and, if you nominate a charismatic candidate, his rallies can draw in new people and energize them.

A party isn't a party unless you run candidates, even when charismatic ones are in short supply. In Santa Cruz we ran a couple serious but unsuccessful campaigns for local office. For Congress and the California legislature, we ran candidates just to use the ballot line and garner any free publicity we could. In 1984 and 1986 it was my turn to be a candidate, so I ran twice against the incumbent Congressman, Democrat Leon Panetta. My votes and the votes cast for the Republican candidate weren't even speedbumps for Panetta's career. He went on to become Clinton's Chief of Staff, Director of the CIA, Director of the Office of Management and Budget, and Secretary of Defense! Later he secured his old seat for his son, Jimmy Panetta.

A few memories of these campaigns stand out. Candidate forums were a waste of time. Few people showed up. Panetta usually sent an aide, sometimes not even that. The couple of times I saw him, about all he had to say was "The people of my district are great people. Our local economy is strong and resilient," and so forth. He was against oil drilling on the coast, so every two years he would save the coast for us again. The truth is that politicians try to avoid discussing the core functions of the federal government found in the constitution. They want "feel good" issues. I received a campaign mailer recently totally given over to my congressman telling me how to protect my property from wildfires—thin gruel compared with the national problems we face and irrelevant to what is supposed to be the work of his office.

During my campaigns, I scored a few television and radio appearances and some newspaper interviews. The newspaper articles would inevitably lead with, "Bill Anderson knows he can't win." This was true, but in their solicitude to assure the public that I was not delusional, they diverted attention from what I was saying.

Community Printers, the local worker-owned printers collective, printed my brochure. Afterword, apparently, they actually read it because they refused to print me additional copies. Of course, no one should be forced to print anything, but I was disappointed by these people who, if they were sincere, must have agreed with much of what I had to say.

*

A significant portion of the faculty at American colleges and universities have dedicated themselves to the task of turning out students who become leftist agitators of some sort. Except among old line Marxists, Lenin and Trotsky have lost most of their appeal as role models. Today, students susceptible to this sort of thing dream (as they prepare themselves for their jobs in the bureaucracy) of being either Saul Alinsky or Rosa Luxembourg. Luxembourg's doomed attempt to create a communist anarchist commune in post-World War One Germany has romantic appeal, particularly as she died a martyr to the cause, but to be an Alinsky seems more practical. He even wrote two books telling you how to do it. Alinsky, who died in 1971, is an admirable figure in some respects, but there is a big problem with his approach, which I can illustrate with one of his stories.

Some students from a Christian College came to him and complained that the administration of the college did not allow them to smoke(!), dance, or drink beer. They wanted these rules repealed. Alinsky's solution was to advise the students to chew gum and then discard the gum on the sidewalks of the school. The students did this, and when the cost of daily gum removal became large, the administration relented and repealed the rules. This action was a success in Alinsky's eyes.

What might the students have done instead? They might have transferred to another school. This is what happens in a free market. People who don't like the terms of an exchange exit. People who like the terms stay, and everyone is happy to the extent that the reality of our differing desires allows. The problem here is that most students don't pay for their own schooling – their parents pay for it. The real beef was between the students and their parents, parents who apparently liked the administration's rules or did not care. This is a problem inherent in any third-party payment for a good or service, and it is hard to get around it when the beneficiary is a child presumed by the parents not to know what's best.

The other thing the students could have done is disobey the rules they objected to. Hold a dance in the quad. Bring a keg. If enough students did this, the administration would likely not expel them, and the rules would be effectively repealed. We might refer to this approach as "self-liquidating disobedience;"

disobedience and repeal are the same action. The deed is the victory. In contrast, shedding gum so that people get it stuck to their shoes is aggression against innocent people. And this tactic can be attached to any goal. Why not use the gum weapon to demand anything that can be imagined?

This is the problem with some of Alinsky's tactics. They can easily become an extortion racket. In fact, some later writers, such as Frances Fox Piven and Richard Cloward, embrace this extension: Be as obnoxious as possible and people will throw money at you to make you stop. But if everyone adopts these tactics, social cooperation begins to break down. We see things like teachers in Mexico burning piles of old tires in the middle of town demanding money. Up to a point and as long as the money holds out, each group can be paid off, but at the cost of the integration of that group into the list of clients of the powerful. Your movement becomes another brick in the edifice of power.

In Alinsky's books, we read about power, but there is no discussion about how a society without power would work. There is struggle, but no vision of voluntary cooperation. Of course, he is under no obligation to provide this, but the lack of a wider perspective limits his access to real solutions. Might an increase in the supply of housing solve some of the problems the rent strike is supposed to address? Might the rent strike reduce the supply of housing in the long run?

Alinsky suggested giving each poor person an ID card that could be used to give him or her exemption from the sales tax on any transaction. Think about the problems this would involve. There is the cost of issuing the cards to the right people. There is the problem of forged cards. There is the possibility that people would use the card and resell the goods on the black market. If you had such a card, you would feel less incentive to raise yourself from poverty.

MY LIBERTARIAN EDUCATION   93

Alinsky comes across as someone you'd like to sit down and swap stories with over a beer. If I could, I'd say to him, "How about this, Saul: How about we burn the sales tax returns, shred the resale cards, dump a trash load of the latest sales tax rulings and regulations onto the desks of the bureaucrats and politicians who wrote them, and fire everyone at the State Board of Equalization?" *That* would be a *real* trumpet for radicals.

*

Looking for any opportunity to reach people when they are paying attention, our Libertarian Party group would distribute leaflets on taxes to people going into the main post office on April 15th. One day I was leafleting by myself on the terrace above the wide apron of the main post office steps. I have long experience of leafleting. Some people seek you out as they walk by, wanting to see what you are handing out. Some appear indifferent, but don't try to avoid you. Usually, these people will take a leaflet if you offer one to them, but not always. Some people go out of their way to avoid you or look hostile. You leave these people alone. And some of the people who walk by are crazy.

That morning, a Black woman came up the stairs and was glad to take the leaflet I offered her. Later, a Black man came up the stairs and began to walk near me with no expression on his face. I offered him a leaflet and he broke into a smile as he took it. Then I saw a young Black man give me an angry look as he mounted the stairs. He didn't make eye contact as he walked by, and I let him pass. As soon as he had passed me, he wheeled around and demanded,

"Why didn't you give me one of those?"

Before I could say anything, he answered his own question,

"You didn't give me one because I'm Black!"

I started to explain that I'd given one to every Black person before him, but he would have none of it.

"Don't give me that. I KNOW ALL ABOUT PEOPLE LIKE YOU!" he said as he stormed off.

This encounter took place a couple decades before the advent of "wokeness." Remembering it now occasions two reflections: First, if you are angry, you *will* find microaggressions. Secondly, saying "I know all about people like you" after ten seconds acquaintance is pretty much the essence of wokeness.

*

The race for the presidency commands the most attention of any political event and has the potential of garnering national media coverage. There was always a lively interest in who our libertarian nominee would be and whether that person would be a good spokesman for the cause. Harry Browne did a good job of selling our ideas when he ran, and Roger MacBride was a thoughtful gentleman, but the outstanding Libertarian Party presidential candidate was Ron Paul, who ran on our ballot line in 1988, twenty years before his first GOP run.

For a third-party candidate to break through to the national media is difficult, so the campaign focused on the hard slog of going from local newspapers to local radio to local television for interviews in the hope that some of it would be run, especially in the small markets.

When Ron Paul arrived in Santa Cruz, I volunteered to be his driver for a day, so he and I rode to places in Monterey, Salinas, and Watsonville where he could give interviews. He was quiet, soft-spoken and polite. There was none of the foul language you sometimes hear from politicians when they are not in public. (It was Nixon's deleted expletives as much as anything that lost him public opinion.) At each stop, I would sit in on Paul's interview and listen. These were so engaging that I once jumped right in and answered the interviewer's question before Ron could say anything. Of course, as soon as we left the building I apologized profusely, but Ron just shrugged, "It's OK. You made a good answer."

"Wow," I thought, "A politician who isn't a narcissistic, egomaniacal control-freak."

Ron Paul's candidacy in the Republican Party presidential primaries of 2008 and 2012 was probably the country's last chance to reform our political system from the top down through national elections. Ron knew what needed to be done. He had a coherent platform, in that each plank was consistent with and reinforced the others. He maintained friendly relations with all his fellow congress members because he knew that he could work with every one of them on at least some issues, and he had the "insider" knowledge of someone who had served on both the Banking Committee and the Foreign Affairs committee. Most important of all, Ron Paul is a man of principle, who voted his convictions rather than the party line. Yet, Republican primary election voters didn't select Paul, the perfect vehicle for overthrowing the Republican Establishment. Instead, four years later, they chose Donald Trump.

Confronting the State II

"Why would anyone *not* take the money?" Jerry asked urgently, "My lawyer and my accountant both say TAKE THE MONEY!" Jerry was opining on the latest "money drop," the Paycheck Protection Program, an engraved invitation to fraud that conferred most of its benefits on people who didn't need it. This was followed by the Employee Retention Tax Credit embarrassment, final proof that Congress doesn't read the bills it passes. Along with these, we had the corporate welfare of the CHIPS Act and the miss-named "Inflation Reduction Act."

Helicopter money that falls from the sky like rain until it inundates the countryside with inflation, long a metaphor taught in Economics 1, has now become a reality. But the point is this: like Jerry, *we can no longer think of a reason not to take the money.* The "res publica" or "public thing" that an ideal republic is supposed to create, has become a mere ATM machine, and it elicits about as much loyalty. This is probably a good thing. The republican ideal was always a myth, and the more of us who step up to take the money, the sooner that myth will be exposed. And, after all, aren't we owed compensation for all we've paid in? Walter Block and others have made arguments to this effect. I don't disagree with them, but doesn't it break a libertarian's heart to take a government check when you can live without it? Better to opt out when you can.

If you can homeschool, you should. If you can forgo social security benefits, you should. If you receive a stimulus check and you have a roof over your head and food in your pantry, consider giving that check to charity. Your vote will no longer be a hostage to threats of budget cuts. Your integrity will strike fear into the hearts of the politicos.

*

There are many ways to slice-and-dice "social class," some of them useful. I recently found one that posits four classes: First, a very small political Elite. Second, a Clerisy composed of people who are paid with a government check or work for a member of the elite and spend at least some of their time spreading statist ideology. Third, a Dependent Class that encompasses most of the rest of the government employees (excepting especially a few "Andre Saharovs"), industries dependent on government largess or special privileges, welfare clients, and many of the people in the private sector who are living paycheck-to-paycheck. Fourth is the Yeomanry, mostly those skilled workers, professionals, and business owners who are in the market sector of the economy. Members of the yeomanry possess that modicum of independence that allows them to risk thinking for themselves and risk taking action without central direction. The purpose of this four-fold division is not to denigrate anyone (most people are honest and want to do what they believe to be right), but rather to point up the important fact that, as a practical matter, *serious* threats to the Elite find their origin and sustenance in the Yeomanry.

The goal of all governments is to destroy the yeomanry by bringing it under control. This can be done in many ways. Subsidies and special privileges may be offered on the one hand, or threats of taxation and costly regulations made on the other. These are functionally equivalent from the point of view of the state. Whatever the approach in a given case, the point is that a narrow cost-and-benefits discussion of any particular government program is less important than the question: "Does this program destroy the independence of yet another group of people?" Over the years, teachers, doctors, and so forth have been fed into the hopper and bureaucratized without enough thought given to this larger consequence.

A totalitarian state, as Mussolini reminded us, is one with "nothing outside the state." The measure of your freedom is taken by answering the question, "How much of your life is outside the state? ... Outside the realm of coercion?"

*

I once participated on a panel on the subject of political action as the lone libertarian alongside three Marxists. Two of the Marxists robotically repeated the party line of their brand of Marxism. But one, Mike Rotkin, a former mayor of Santa Cruz, spoke like someone who had actually done some thinking. Rotkin said that he was sympathetic with the radical liberal-libertarian-anarchist position, but that this position rested on a fundamental error: It supposed that the state might leave us alone. "The state will *never* leave you alone," he said. Therefore, any movement that isn't constantly thinking about how to gain and hold state power for itself is wasting its time. If strategizing over power crowds out other considerations, so be it.

How to secure your independence? How to be left alone? How to accomplish these tasks without helping someone seize power? One option is to simply ignore the state; go ahead and do what you want, as long as it's peaceful and honest, and hope you don't get caught. This is hardly living in freedom, and it is not likely to bring about fundamental change. Even in economies where tax evasion is widespread and large numbers of people transact business in alternative currencies, the state seems to retain much of its power. (Look at Argentina.) Open defiance of the state will only get you arrested. Disobedience can work only when large numbers of people join in and a considerable number of the rest sympathize with your cause. Using the law to help you is another strategy. File lawsuits in self-defense and hope for success in court. Public interest law firms put this strategy within reach, if you can find an organization that will take your case. The grave flaw in the lawsuit strategy is that it makes the government, which includes the courts, the judge of its own case.

*

About twenty years ago, I served on a jury for the first time. A young woman was being prosecuted for "impeding the police in the performance of their duty." On the face of it, this seemed improbable. She was a slip of a girl, and two burly police officers had her restrained. What had she done? Parked in their stalled car on the side of the road, she had advised one of the two men with her that he was not required to take a breathalyzer test because he had not been driving the car. Ironically, the young woman was a Law Enforcement major at Cabrillo College, and she was simply repeating something she had recently learned in class. Too bad! The prosecutor said that her words were a threat to the police!

We acquitted her by a vote of 10 to 2. I was distressed by the attitude of the 2. One of them said, "Just do whatever the police say and you won't have a problem," which in this case would have meant not speaking up about your rights. After the trial, the young woman decided to change her major.

This case brought home to me how precious is our right to trial by jury. This right to defend ourselves before a jury that judges our guilt or innocence is magnified when the jury is also given the task of *judging the justice of the law*. This power of the jury is referred to as "jury rights" or "jury nullification." The idea is that, if a jury finds the law under which a defendant is charged to be an unjust law, it can find the defendant "not guilty," even if the defendant violated the letter of the law. Most jury rights advocates limit its scope to the criminal law. "Crimes against the state" may be nullified as crimes. Civil cases, in which one person or group alleges actionable harm caused by another, would not be nullifiable because harm, if proven, should be redressed, and the plaintiff would have ample grounds to dismiss a juror who did not think so.

Recognizing jury rights would increase the power of juries. Of all legal entities, the jury is the one least likely to establish a tyranny. Its authority extends only to the case at hand, and as soon as the jury's power is exercised, that jury is dissolved. Would chaos result from jury nullification? No, not as long as a predictable civil law is functioning, whether provided by the state or not. (Competition among legal codes is likely to do the best job of defining actionable harms.) At the limit, jury nullification would produce a society in which there is no criminal law and all law is civil. Crimes that do harm would be tried as civil cases.

Jury nullification is promoted by the Fully Informed Jury Association. One of this organization's projects is to distribute flyers about jury rights at courthouses. This produces a free speech case and publicity for the cause whenever one of their pamphleteers is arrested. Once, when I was in court sitting with a pool of potential jurors waiting to be called, someone brought the judge one of these flyers that had been found outside. The judge, holding up the flyer, proceeded to give us an angry lecture. He would not tolerate anyone bringing this "garbage" into his courtroom! I was not called that day, and I don't know what the case was about. A couple of years later I was in another jury pool. This time I was called up for examination by the opposing counsels. I brought my copy of Clay Conrad's book *Jury Nullification* that day and had been ostentatiously reading it with the title clearly visible. One of the lawyers asked, "Mr. Anderson, I see you're reading about jury nullification. Are you prepared to accept the judge's instructions in this case?" It was a civil case, so I explained that I was prepared to accept the judge's instructions. Both lawyers questioned me, and they kept coming back to this question of jury rights. Unlike the judge I had encountered the last time, this one seemed amused by this line of questioning. It was as if each lawyer was signaling to the other, "Are you going to burn one of your allowed objections to get rid of this nut, or am I going to have to?" Finally, one of them said "Mr. Anderson is excused." As I walked out the judge said, "Well, Mr. Anderson, now you'll have more time to read your book." And so I did.

The 19th century American lawyer and abolitionist Lysander Spooner was the most famous and influential proponent of jury rights, partly because he wanted to nullify the Fugitive Slave Law. But Spooner also imagined nullification of tax enforcement. This points up the limits of a jury strategy; if you're before an administrative agency or in tax court, you're not going to get a jury trial. Still, the jury deserves respect as a place where the defense of our liberties is put into the hands of ordinary people.

Saving the Books

"Libertarianism will be the dominate political ideology among intellectuals in my lifetime," Joe Fuhrig, an adjunct professor of economics, told me around 1984. Sadly, Joe died a few years later, but even if he had lived a normal span (in his late 70s by now), his prophecy was not fulfilled. It didn't seem crazy at the time. Leonard Liggio had recently told us he was heartened by the fact that libertarians were actually being hired for tenure-track positions. But Liggio also liked to caution us by quoting Rand: "It's earlier than you think."

For years after graduating from UCSC, I would occasionally go to the campus bookstore to see what the students were being assigned. What I saw was not encouraging. Books supportive of free market and libertarian ideas were seldom to be found. Why not? By the mid-1970s economics was widely acknowledged to be in crisis. "We need," economists said, "a new post-Keynesian paradigm." Free market thought was getting a hearing. Uncovering the unintended consequences of government intervention became a pursuit that rivaled the usual search for market failure. Public Choice became a field. Stagflation provided the backdrop for a general disillusionment with current ways of thinking.

Yet this pro-freedom intellectual ferment came to naught in terms of influence on policy or in academia. (Those leftists who say that we've been living under a free-market-reign-of-terror since the Reagan Administration are beyond delusional.) Why has support for freedom made no overall progress? Was it affirmative action and the raising of ethnic and gender studies to the status of majors, shifting the focus of study to identity politics? (Many who choose these majors become political commissars.) Was it the predilection of the "red diaper babies," students whose parents had been communists in the 1930s, for academic careers, and their ruthlessness in advancing their cadres? Or was it the sheer amount of money thrown at the universities in tax support, grants, and aid for students that overwhelmed any questioning of statism?

I noticed the first stirrings of political correctness in Spring 1974 when, in one of my classes, a couple of female students wanted to ditch the day's lesson to speak about how using male pronouns to talk about humans in general oppresses women. This apparently happened in a lot of classes that week, suggesting a coordinated effort, where they fanned out with their marching orders from a central gathering. I graduated a few weeks later, and didn't give identity politics on campus much thought until 1988, when I first heard the words "politically correct" ("PC" for short)," from a couple of students I knew. "You hear that phrase all the time on campus," they said. It referred to a network of people dedicated to helping each other's careers and shutting out others.

By 2017, I noticed that the core courses at each college at UCSC, courses every freshman is required to take, were now dedicated to indoctrinating the new students with the Official Ideology of who is oppressing whom and how every cultural artifact serves that end. For example, one of the assigned books was *Is Everyone Really Equal?: An Introduction to Key Concepts in Social Justice Education* by Ozlem Sensoy and Robin DiAngelo.

Liberal systems punish people when they aggress against others. Totalitarian systems focus on thoughtcrime. Liberal systems encourage debate and discussion. Totalitarian systems are founded on groupthink. Just as Chairman Mao sought to shore-up his rule by unleashing his Red Guards, our own elites have unleashed the cancel culture on us to cow us into silence and to divert attention from what they are up to. It's the Chinese Cultural Revolution all over again, lacking only the Little Red Book and Mao's Pink and Radiant Face.

My day job was far removed from what was happening on campus. And my reading: the Austrian economists, "Old Right" Libertarians, classical liberal philosophers and historians, and work put out by free-market think tanks, was far removed from what was being taught on campus. There was little opportunity for me to engage in serious discussion with anyone about these ideas. Sometimes, while dealing with another pile of invoices on my desk, I tried to brainstorm how I could somehow engage the students—perhaps help write independent studies proposals or start a campus student organization.

It is notoriously difficult to establish and maintain a student club that does serious work. Only a few students will be interested. Any enthusiasm displayed at the beginning of the quarter dissipates when papers are due and finals loom. Each year a large portion of your membership graduates. A club devoted to political ideas faces the temptations of getting involved in electoral politics, which puts an end to serious thinking, or of inviting "provocateurs" to campus instead of serious scholars. The most successful libertarian club at UCSC was active in 1988. They published a campus newspaper and hosted a visit by Ron Paul. Hans Eicholz, who later earned his PhD in history, wrote a book on Jefferson, and went on to work for Liberty Fund, was a member. So was Bretigne Schaffer, the daughter of libertarian law professor and writer Butler Schaffer. Betigne went on to become a journalist, working for a time for the Asian edition of the Wall Street Journal.

I thought this might be the beginning of a trend. Second-generation libertarians would soon arrive on campus, I hoped. They would challenge the faculty and start asking pointed questions about why certain authors were not being assigned. Why for example, was Marx assigned to U.S. students 32,376 times versus only 773 times for Mises, according to the running total compiled at Open Syllabus? Alas, dissent from the campus consensus became more muted rather than more vocal. Classes challenging the consensus became harder to find. In 2010, I asked the head of the economics department whether the students were ever assigned readings from the Austrian School and was told, "Only in a history of economic thought class." Then I looked at the course catalog and saw that no history of economic thought class was offered.

This is not an arcane matter. Students graduate with a degree in economics without ever hearing any questioning of the need for a central bank and never reading about the case for a gold or commodity standard. Fractional reserve banking and fiat money are taken for granted. An understanding of interest rates as a price that arises naturally out of time preference is replaced by the view that interest rates are something the authorities make up.

Macroeconomics is corrupt. The Federal Reserve, with more than 23,000 total employees, employs hundreds of economists and distributes millions of dollars in research grants each year. Economists work for banks that are members of the Fed. Economists on the Fed's payroll sit on the boards of the prestigious journals and determine who is published there. The power to grant or deny tenure helps the establishment police the system. The system they guard transfers wealth to the banks, to the national security state, to the political patronage machines and to the 1 percent, who have the most access to newly printed money and who benefit from asset price inflation. Economics has become econometrics, mathematical modeling of the complex system that is the modern economy, a "science" that is notoriously unreliable.

I can't help but notice that climate science and epidemiology share certain characteristics with macroeconomics. They all have interest groups that profit from a certain set of policies. All have government bureaucracies that dispense the lion's share of research grants. And all advance computer models of highly complex systems as science. I don't know enough about these subjects to have an informed opinion, but I do know that approaching official pronouncements with skepticism is not irrational or unscientific.

*

In the summer of 2010, I shed most of my business responsibilities and was looking for things to do. Besides volunteering for a couple of organizations, I began to speak to clubs and high school classes on various topics. But I wanted to do more. By the end of 2012, a series of serendipitous connections brought me to the home of Faye Crosby, the Provost of Cowell College, UCSC. Faye was interested in giving the students more contact with alumni who had had careers outside academia – 60-year-olds with experience in the real world talking with 20-year-olds was the idea. She was open to allowing alums without PhDs to teach "for credit" classes with a faculty member sponsor. During the course of our dinner table conversation, I satisfied her that 1) I am not a crazy person and 2) I can put together a serious reading list. So, I was "hired," and in January 2013 my academic career began. For six months out of the year for the next seven years, I taught students at UCSC under the sponsorship of the provost. Since I was an unpaid volunteer and my classes couldn't be used to satisfy major requirements, the departments and the faculty didn't care what I was doing. And I could teach the small classes and the two-unit classes some students were looking for that didn't repay a professor's time.

"An Introduction to Anarchism" was by far my most popular class. A few students took it because they wanted two units. Some relished the "shock value" of telling their parents that they were studying anarchism. Most were genuinely curious. I always had one or two students who were into communist anarchism or some form of antimarket, stateless collectivism. I covered this area by assigning and sympathetically discussing Peter Kropotkin and Emma Goldman, but when these students discovered my main interest was in the individualists and the market anarchists, they would sometimes complain that I was not teaching "real anarchism."

I think they missed the point. No matter what your political ideology, the interesting question to explore is this: What sort of social order arises when there is no monopoly provider of law? The market anarchists and their market-savvy critics address this question head-on, which is what makes their writings interesting. The collectivist anarchists evade the question, either by becoming utopians and assuming an end to scarcity, including scarcity of knowledge, or by embracing primitivism and projecting a society so simple that law has not yet emerged from custom.

My biggest disappointment was that there were a couple of years where my anarchism students ditched class in solidarity with striking graduate students who were blocking the entrance to the campus. In other words, they were supporting more state education and another public employee union. Not exactly anarchism.

The other politics class I taught was "Classical Liberalism in the Twentieth Century," which attracted a handful of students, all of whom were seriously interested in the subject. (The syllabi for all my classes are provided in the appendix.) My class on "Mises's *Human Action*" also attracted a small number of serious students for a close reading of this great treatise.

My most popular class after "Anarchism" was "Austrian Business Cycle Theory," (Yes, it needed a catchier title.), which presented an alternative macroeconomics. A few of these students became real enthusiasts, recommending the class to others and formulating some pointed questions to ask their professors. A final class I was preparing, on "Classical Liberalism to 1914," was derailed by Covid and the subject's daunting scope.

I recommend teaching to anyone serious about learning. Teaching a class means rereading the books multiple times, scanning for new material, thinking about the subject a lot, writing about it so that it is presented in a coherent and understandable manner, and finally, subjecting yourself to questions and comments that will help you to see the subject in new ways. When you teach a class multiple times, you should find yourself stripping away rhetoric and jargon, defining your terms more and more precisely, examining the soundness of each step of an argument, and listening closely to objections. I learned a lot from my students. More than a few were clearly brighter than me. My claim to be their teacher rested on the forty five years of reading, thinking and experiencing I had on them. I never felt like an "imposter" when I stood before my students, but I never ceased to feel amazed when they showed up week after week to hear what I had to say.

*

Back in the late 1930s, when interest in classical liberalism was at low ebb, one free-market economist told his friends, "The best we can hope to do is save the books. Maybe, like a time capsule, they will be rediscovered someday and speak to that future time." There has been an efflorescence of classical liberal/libertarian thought since the 1930s. So why does it feel like we are *still just saving the books?* The campus is almost universally hostile to markets. People often don't even bother to argue against markets. They just sneer at them.

I asked Joe Fuhrig once what he thought of the unionization of college faculty. He replied that it was a good thing because it was one more sign that higher education is a dying industry. If Joe were alive today, he would smile at his prescience. We've all seen the list: students who don't graduate, student debt, students who can't write at college level even after they've passed the freshman English requirement, graduate students who can't find jobs, undergrads unprepared for the job market, more use of adjuncts, more and more administrators, less and less tolerance of dissenting opinions, and more classes that are not offered in person.

But my disillusionment reached a new level when colleges required healthy twenty-year-olds *with natural immunity* to take an experimental vaccine if they wanted to stay in school. The people who run most universities care only about staying on the good side of those who dispense grants. The students mean nothing to them.

Does it make sense to embark on a "long march through the institutions" when those institutions are decaying? I would probably go back to teaching a few students at UCSC, if given the opportunity, but what I would really like to do is find and teach those students who want to learn and are wise enough to pursue learning outside college.

"What Did You Do During the Coup, Daddy?"

The U.S. Political Class went insane in three steps. First, when the Soviet Union dissolved, the U.S. elite decided that it now ruled the world and could, for example, remake the Middle East to its liking. Secondly, when the housing bubble collapsed and the Fed created a massive amount of bank reserves without igniting much consumer level inflation, the elite thought it had found a way to create unlimited wealth at no cost. Finally, when the voters expressed their independence by electing Donald Trump, the elites decided they needed to be prepared to do whatever had to be done to make themselves unassailable.

In the epigraph to one of the chapters of Friedrich Hayek's *The Road to Serfdom,* Hayek quotes an observer in Germany in 1931 as saying "All antiliberal forces are combining against everything that is liberal." That seems to be what is happening in the United States today. Socialists and bankers, leftists and the military industrial complex, the woke brigades and large corporations, black lives matter and the national security state – these groups have their differences, but they all oppose traditional American liberty. We even have our "Brown Shirts" (Antifa) and our "Red Guards" (the Woke.) "These times have the feel of a slow-motion coup d'état," I heard someone say.

How will it end? How will the lines of political opposition be defined? Trump versus anti-Trump? Republicans versus Democrats? Left versus Right? Race versus Race? The One Percent versus the Ninety Nine Percent? The best guess is that events will come down to a showdown between the centralizers and the decentralizers.

Since the Civil War, the trend in American history has been the concentration of power in Washington DC. Whatever the causes of this, it has certainly been facilitated by the federalization of the money and banking system and the increased capacity of that system to create money and use it to buy the federal government's debt. First, we had the National Banking Act, enacted during the Civil War. Then we got a central bank when the Federal Reserve was established in 1913. After World War II, the Bretton Woods Agreement gave the world a limited gold exchange standard with the dollar as the key reserve currency. This morphed into a pure fiat dollar standard in 1971. *Each shift in the monetary set-up made it easier for the authorities to create dollars.* And the more dollars created, the more federal debt that could be sold to the monetary authorities. We now have debts, entitlement promises, pension promises, and military obligations that can't all be honored.

As long as sufficient resources can be squeezed out of the fiat dollar by creating more of them, the system can be maintained. Since fiat money is backed by nothing solid and carries the moral hazard of costless production, the question arises: "How has the fiat dollar managed to last this long?" The first answer was the Petrodollar. Saudi Arabia was persuaded to price its oil in dollars and use its dollar earnings to buy U.S. weapons, make deposits in U.S. banks and buy U.S. investments. Any country that does not price its oil in dollars became our enemy. Secondly, as the United States issued more and more dollars, our trading partners saw their currencies appreciate, jeopardizing their exports, so they issued more of their own currencies to stabilize the exchange rate, buying dollars or U.S. treasury securities to hold in the vaults of their central banks. This gave the U.S. empire a financial base. We can import real goods while exporting "pieces of paper," dollars or dollar securities. (This is why the nation that prints the world's reserve currency will run a trade deficit. Trying to fix that deficit with tariffs is futile.)

Finally, as long as U.S. taxes are paid in dollars there will be a demand to hold dollars to meet those payments as they come due. Left anarchist David Graeber argues that this "taxation demand" for money is the only kind of money demand that exists, and that there is no demand for money as a medium of exchange. This larger claim is mistaken, but he is correct that "taxation demand" is an important reason why fiat money has persisted for so long.

Now there is too much debt. Too many borrowers (including the government) are dependent on low interest rates, and trouble comes when rates rise. Monetary expansion that enriched the one percent by inflating asset prices is filtering out to consumers. Additional money is being handed out to consumers in the form of "stimulus." Rising consumer prices are the result.

It's the printing press in Washington that undergirds federal power. The military industrial complex, the empire of bases, the national security state, our financial institutions, the political patronage machines, academia, and the transfer payments that keep the herd from stampeding all depend on the Fed's ability to squeeze a little more juice out of the fiat dollar.

The best evidence that the end game of fiat money has begun is the fact that they have given it a name: "The Great Reset." The goal of the Reset is to make the transition to a new monetary system without the elite losing its power. In their dreams, money will remain fiat money, so the power to create money will not be surrendered, but all bank accounts will be (in reality, if not in name) at a single monopoly bank, the Fed. Cash will be outlawed. With no need for reserves to either meet the demand for currency or settle interbank clearings, increases in the money supply can be accomplished without the clumsy mechanism of independent banks managing their reserve balances and without the government having to share the profits of money creation with those banks. All credit will be allocated by a supreme council of politically appointed bureaucrats and business leaders (an ultimate goal of Keynes), so interest rates can be any numbers they care to make up. Your account will be credited each month with your guaranteed income supplement, and debited each month for your share of "investment," the new name for taxation. All your transactions will be monitored. Your tax returns will be prepared for you by the IRS. Unapproved expenditures can be blocked, giving the authorities control over your behavior. If you become a political dissident, your account might be closed, cutting you off from the payments system entirely when the social credit score that measures your obedience falls too low. This is the "full package" scenario. How it actually plays out is unpredictable.

This "revolution from above" might be accomplished under a number of different banners: Debt cancellation, restoring retirement account balances to what they were on some previous date, equity or reparations, a guaranteed income, micromanaging our behavior in order to save the environment, or controlling people's healthcare decisions.

*

The notion that our liberty will be protected by a system of checks-and-balances operating in Washington is a joke, and there are no social institutions outside the state powerful enough to organize effective resistance. We are left with federalism as our best alternative – in which some of the state governments might "push back" against federal decrees in a crisis. States and smaller jurisdictions reluctant to embrace secession might be willing to practice nullification, the nonenforcement of unconstitutional laws. The key to successful nullification is that state employees can't be commandeered to help enforce federal legislation, and there are not enough federal employees to do this job by themselves.

Legal marijuana in defiance of federal law is the most recent example of successful nullification. Nullification's progress on other issues can be followed at the Tenth Amendment Center. While many worthy efforts are underway, the three most consequential proposals are these: 1) Defend the Guard. States would not deploy their National Guard troops abroad without a declaration of war. 2) Tax Escrow Accounts. Each state legislature would create a commission to receive all the federal taxes paid in their state. Only those amounts judged by the commission as used for constitutional purposes would be remitted to Washington. 3) Legal Tender. States would affirm that gold and silver are legal tender. Sales and capital gains taxes on gold and silver would be repealed, and gold banks that offer 100% gold accounts would be allowed to operate, providing an alternative payment system. There has been some encouraging progress on the legal tender front.

*

This is the point where the usual litany of exhortations appears: turn off your television, educate yourself, set a good example, talk with your friends and neighbors, etc. One can even go further and say: create alternative institutions and support them, etc. That may be enough. I hope we never get to the point where our liberty depends on persuading a young man in a tank to open the hatch and come out and join us.

Narratives

"To live over people's lives is nothing unless we live over their perceptions, live over their growth, the change, the varying intensity of the same – since it was by these things they themselves lived." – Henry James

"Each man is haunted by the memory of some troubling fact, on which all his logic focuses. You may believe he is expounding a whole theory to you; he is really trying to justify an hour of his life." – Benjamin Constant

"We tell ourselves stories in order to live." – Joan Didion

"Dixi et salvavi animam meam." [I have spoken and thus saved my soul.]

Had I been born in the hills of Kentucky, I would likely have been taught from my earliest years to hate the coal company, probably with good reason. But to carry that conflict with me for life as a template for understanding society would have stunted my education.

We all have our cognitive biases. I am wont to find among people in small competitive businesses and those professionals who have managed to maintain their independence the last repositories of Republican Virtue, and I'm too quick to dismiss those placed otherwise who disagree with me as either assimilated to the regime or hopelessly confused. I need to remind myself to appreciate more the virtues and potential of others. All of us, at some point, pass judgement on the human race. My verdict is that people are both better and worse than we imagine.

The universality of cognitive bias should not be allowed to lead us to the conclusion that all points of view are "valid" and hence worthy of respect as "true" in some sense that makes everyone's point of view true. I can understand why a son of European immigrants growing up in Detroit or Chicago in the 1930s might believe that the Social Security Act and the National Labor Relations Act were the two greatest pieces of legislation in the history of the world. I can both understand why he believes that *and* declare him to be wrong. I understand why someone who has made his or her entire career in government service might believe that the path to prosperity is to raise taxes and push everyone into a union. It may have worked for them, so far, but it doesn't create an economy any more than Mao's Great Leap Forward, Stalin's Five Year Plan, or Hitler's campaign of conquest and plunder created economies.

Narratives motivate us to act in a certain way by giving those acts meaning. Every political community has a founding narrative that locates sovereignty and justifies it. Opposition narratives often find the lever of history in a chosen class or group. Narratives can appeal to our noblest impulses or to our basest ones. Political narratives often rely for their force on that "systematic organization of hatreds" Henry Adams found in practical politics.

Narratives explain the past and may predict the future. Failure to predict can upend our understanding of what has been going on. When the last helicopter left Saigon, I said to myself, "That's it. The United States won't be in any more wars in my lifetime. The people won't stand for it." Soon after the Berlin Wall was chiseled and sledgehammered down, my father and I were driving past an armory that had an old army tank parked in front of it. My father pointed to the tank and said "We won't need those anymore. Maybe we are at the beginning of a Golden Age!"

The Nazis were dust and communism had collapsed, yet we didn't come home. The Republic was not restored. Thirty years on and from Serbia, to Sudan, Somalia, Iraq, Afghanistan, Syria, Libya, Yemen and the proxy war we're waging in Ukraine, and whether with bombs or ground troops or drones, there has been continual violence on the periphery of the empire. Must we now revise our narratives and say that the anti-Vietnam War movement didn't run deep as an *anti-war* movement, and that the Cold War was about something other than defeating communism?

It is easy to conclude that there is no progress. Humans by nature are prone to make the same errors. They fall prey to the same manipulations, and each generation is born ignorant and vulnerable. The permanence of war and preparation for war is the most egregious example of this lack of progress. The hardiness of economic fallacies is another. (Surely Sisyphus was a free-market economist.) It is easy to fall into pessimism, and once pessimism takes hold, the narrative turns from "saving the world" to "saving souls" and eventually to one's own salvation.

Soul-saving speech is either Confession or Witness. Confession says, "I am responsible. I am in need of forgiveness." Witness says, "I will speak the truth, come what may." Today a good time to examine our own lives, renounce the powers of this world, and prepare for whatever witness the coming years require.

Appendix

On Being Doctrinaire

Common sense seems to dictate that moderate viewpoints are correct, the fruit of some sort of collective wisdom, but history teaches otherwise. Moderation is a moving target. Today's extreme views become tomorrow's consensus. The reasonable person of today is tomorrow the subject of ridicule. Views that seem extreme should not be dismissed before they are given careful examination.

Libertarians are sometimes criticized for being relentlessly negative about the state. It seems so unreasonable. But in fact, anti-statism is eminently reasonable. It is founded on two key insights: 1) A monopoly provider of law will produce bad law because bad law is a product that can be sold; and 2) The institution empowered to acquire its revenue through force and fraud will eventually swallow everything.

*

When I was younger, I could easily name our two California Senators, along with my Congressman, State Senator, Assemblyman, County Supervisor and City Council members. One day a few years ago, though my memory is otherwise fine, I couldn't remember the name of one of the California U.S. Senators. Searching my memory, I knew who my congressman was, but I couldn't remember the names of my state senator or assemblyperson. For the rest, I could give only a couple of names and was not sure whether they were still in office.

Bemused, I said to myself, "I guess I'm through with these people."

Politics or Culture?

The current wisdom is that "politics is downstream from culture." I'm not so sure. Following Robert Higgs, politics uses crises and fear to create institutions of mass obedience. Once these institutions are in place, the resulting incentives bend ideology, and ultimately culture, to the needs of power. This, in turn, makes the next round of political institution building easier to accomplish, at least until the whole thing collapses under the weight of the laws of economics and unintended consequences. The "wild card" here is technology. The printing press, firearms, the machine gun, the mass media, the bomb, the pill, the computer, the Internet, biotechnology – these are up for grabs as drivers of liberation or bondage.

On Intellectual Fragility

Some of what people describe as "emotional fragility" may actually be intellectual fragility, an emotional reaction to being unable to rigorously defend one's views. Intellectual fragility can be countered in only one way: by studying your opponent's views. "Listen to all points of view" is more than a bromide; it is *vitally necessary.* The importance of having your opponent's arguments down cold has been recognized by serious thinkers from John Stuart Mill to the Society of Jesus. (Though this admirable virtue of the Jesuits seems to have been lost in recent years, according to Walter Block and Thomas DiLorenzo.)

All my life, I have been surrounded by intelligent people, in person and in the media, who disagree with me. Being in the minority feels completely normal, even comfortable. Any discomfort I feel spurs me to do more reading and thinking, sometimes followed by a confession of ignorance or a modification of my position.

Those who could – who were encouraged – to dismiss dissenters out of hand as ignorant or evil or both, can't handle it when a serious person makes a serious argument. They are likely to reach for the "cancel" button, especially when egged on by the work of German Marxist philosophers who see every difference of opinion as a street fight in 1932 Berlin.

My Syllabi

I developed four classes and taught each one several times. Most of the time they were offered as two-unit classes that met once a week. They could be taken pass/fail or graded.

One class was a close reading of Mises' *Human Action*. We used the scholar's edition supplemented with reading the *Human Action Study Guide* by Robert Murphy. I asked the students to write at least two pages a week for all but the first and last weeks. They were to discuss any aspect of that week's readings. Since this class would have only two to four students, there was a lot of classroom discussion.

My second economics class was "Austrian Business Cycle Theory." We began by reading Murray Rothbard's essay "What Has Government Done to Our Money?" The main text was *Money, Bank Credit and Economic Cycles* by Jesus Huerta De Soto. This was supplemented by reading chapters three and four of Roger Garrison's *Time and Money: The Macroeconomics of Capital Structure*. Two essays completed the reading: "A Reformulation of Austrian Business Cycle Theory in Light of the Financial Crisis" by Joseph Salerno and "The Marginal Efficiency of Capital" by Edward Fuller. These essays can be found at mises.org. We had a mid-term and a final. Both were "take home." The mid-term question was: "What is interest and what is the economic function of interest rates?" For the final I asked: "What happens when consumers reduce their consumption and save?" and "What happens when banks expand credit by issuing fiduciary media?" I told the students which pages of the reading would be the most helpful. This class would attract two to five students.

My first politics class was "Classical Liberalism in the Twentieth Century." We read the following books and essays: "The Rise, Fall and Renaissance of Classical Liberalism" by Ralph Raico; "Left and Right: The Prospects for Liberty" by Murray Rothbard; "The Intellectuals and Socialism" by Friedrich Hayek; *Liberalism* by Ludwig von Mises; "Economic Calculation in the Socialist Commonwealth" by Mises; "The Use of Knowledge in Society" by Hayek; *The Road to Serfdom* by Hayek; *Economics in One Lesson* by Henry Hazlitt; *The People's Pottage* by Garet Garrett; "What Has Government Done to Our Money?" by Rothbard; *Anarchy, State and Utopia* by Robert Nozick; *Simple Rules for a Complex World* by Richard Epstein; "Human Rights as Property Rights" by Rothbard; "The Atavism of Social Justice" by Hayek; "Oratorio of the Lost Generation" by Robert Nisbet; "Anatomy of the State" by Rothbard; and "Classical Liberalism's Impossible Dream" by Robert Higgs. To make this much reading manageable, I advised the students which portions of the Garrett, Nozick and Epstein books they could skip over. If I had had more time, I would have added works by Ayn Rand and James Buchanan. Students wrote a short mid-term paper to keep them on track and allow me to assess their writing skills, and a final paper. They could write about anything they wanted as long as it related to the subject of the class. This class would attract two to four students.

My second politics class was "An Introduction to Anarchism." We began with "Anatomy of the State" by Rothbard and "A Theory of the Origin of the State" by Robert Carneiro. Then *In Defense of Anarchism* by Robert Paul Wolff, "On the Duty of Civil

Disobedience" by Henry David Thoreau and "The Right to Ignore the State" by Herbert Spencer. Most of the remaining readings were found in Edward Stringham's anthology *Anarchy and the Law*, specifically the chapters that cover Lysander Spooner, Voltairine de Cleyre, Benjamin Tucker, American History, classic anarcho-capitalist pieces by Rothbard, Friedman and the Tannehills, public goods and national defense, John Hasnas's important essay "The Myth of the Rule of Law," and more. We also read Tucker's "State Socialism and Anarchism," "Anarchist Communism: Its Basis and Principles" by Peter Kropotkin, and "Anarchism: What it Really Stands For" by Emma Goldman. If I were to teach this class again, I would retitle it "Individualist Anarchism," drop the works by Kropotkin, Goldman and Wolff, and add *The Problem of Political Authority: An Examination of the Right to Coerce and the Duty to Obey* by Michael Huemer, and maybe add something from the anthology *The Voluntary City*, edited by Beito, Gordon and Tabarrok. It's not that I don't enjoy discussing the merits and demerits of communist anarchism; it's just that there is no time for them if I include Huemer. In any case, the UCSC politics department offers a course on the collectivist anarchists. Unfortunately for the students, you have to be a politics major to take it. The students were asked to write a paper on any aspect of anarchism that interested them. I would ask for a rough draft of this paper by the sixth or seventh week. My anarchism class typically attracted 10 to 20 students.

About the Author

Bill Anderson was born an early/mid Boomer to a loving family in Northern California that owned a farm, which makes him lucky, but not privileged.

He spent thirty four years in the trenches of small business and has remained a part of that world. He did enough reading to qualify to teach classes to undergraduates for seven years as a volunteer tutor, which is somewhere below the lowest rung of academia.

He thinks it likely that historians a thousand years from now will refer to the 21st century as Late Antiquity II.

His wife and daughter are the joy and balm of his life.

Made in the USA
Middletown, DE
22 January 2025